The Market Research Society

With over 8,000 members in more than 50 countries, The Market Research Society (MRS) is the world's largest international membership organization for professional researchers and other engaged in (or interested in) marketing, social or opinion research.

It has a diverse membership of individual researchers within agencies, independent consultancies, client-side organizations, and the academic community, and from all levels of seniority and job functions.

All MRS members agree to comply with the MRS Code of Conduct (see Appendix 2), which is supported by the Codeline advisory service and a range of specialist guidelines on best practice.

MRS offers various qualifications and membership grades, as well as training and professional development resources to support these. It is the official awarding body in the UK for vocational qualifications in market research.

MRS is a major supplier of publications and information services, conferences and seminars and many other meeting and networking opportunities for researchers.

MRS is 'the voice of the profession' in its media relations and public affairs activities on behalf of professional research practitioners, and aims to achieve the most favourable climate of opinions and legislative environment for research.

The Market Research Society
15 Northburgh Street, London EC1V 0JR
Telephone: 44 20 7490 4911
Fax: 44 20 7490 0608
e-mail: info@marketresearch.org.uk
website: www.mrs.org.uk

MARKET RESEARCH IN PRACTICE SERIES

Published in association with The Market Research Society
Consultant Editors: David Barr and Robin J Birn

Kogan Page has joined forces with The Market Research Society (MRS) to publish this unique series of books designed to cover the latest developments in market research thinking and practice.

The series provides up-to-date knowledge on the techniques of market research and customer insight and best practice in implementing them. It also shows the contribution market research and customer information management techniques can make to helping organizations of all kinds in shaping their strategy, structure, customer focus and value creation.

The series consists of several essential guides that focus on the core skills developed in the MRS training and qualifications programmes (www.mrs.org.uk). It provides practical advice and case studies on how to plan, use, act on and follow-up research, and on how to combine it with other sources of information to develop deep insights into customers.

Fully international in scope of content, its readership is also from all over the world. The series is designed not only for specialist market researchers, but also for all those involved in developing and using deeper insights into their customers – marketers in all disciplines, including planning, communications, brand management, and interactive marketers.

Other titles in the series:
Business to Business Market Research, Ruth McNeil
Consumer Insight, Merlin Stone
The Effective Use of Market Research, Robin J Birn
Market Intelligence: How and why organizations use market research, Martin Callingham
Market Research in Practice: A guide to the basics, Paul Hague, Nick Hague & Carol-Ann Morgan
Questionnaire Design, Ian Brace
Researching Customer Satisfaction and Loyalty, Paul Szwarc

Kogan Page Ltd
120 Pentonville Road
London N1 9JN
Tel: 020 7278 0433
www.kogan-page.co.uk

MRS. MARKET RESEARCH IN PRACTICE

EMPLOYEE RESEARCH

HOW TO INCREASE EMPLOYEE INVOLVEMENT THROUGH CONSULTATION

PETER GOUDGE

KOGAN PAGE

London and Philadelphia

First published in Great Britain and the United States in 2006 by Kogan Page Limited

120 Pentonville Road
London N1 9JN
United Kingdom
www.kogan-page.co.uk

525 South 4th Street, #241
Philadelphia PA 19147
USA

© Peter Goudge, 2006

ISBN 0 7494 4540 8

British Library Cataloging-in-Publication Data

A CIP record for this book is available from the British Library.

Library of Congress Cataloging-in-Publication Data

Goudge, Peter.
    Employee research : how to increase employee involvement through consultation / Peter Goudge.
        p. cm.
    Includes bibliographical references and index.
    ISBN 0-7494-4540-8
    1. Employee attitude surveys. 2. Employees—Attitudes—Research. 3. Job satisfaction—Research. 4. Organizational commitment—Research. 5. Personnel management—Research. I. Title.
    HF5549.5.A83G68 2006
    658.3'145—dc22

                                                                2006001654

Typeset by Digital Publishing Solutions

Printed and bound in the United States by Thomson-Shore, Inc

Contents

The editorial board

SERIES EDITORS

David Barr has been Director General of The Market Research Society since July 1997. He previously spent over 25 years in business information services and publishing. He has held management positions with Xerox Publishing Group, the British Tourist Authority and Reed International plc. His experience of market research is therefore all on the client side, having commissioned many projects for NPD and M&A purposes. A graduate of Glasgow and Sheffield Universities, David Barr is a Fellow of the Chartered Management Institute and a Fellow of The Royal Society of Arts.

Robin J Birn has been marketing and market research practitioner for over 25 years. In 1985 Robin set up Strategy, Research and Action Ltd, a market research company for the map, atlas and travel guide sector, and the book industry. In 2004 he was appointed Head of Consultation and Research at the Institute of Chartered Accountants of England and Wales. He is a Fellow of The Market Research Society and a Fellow of the Chartered Institute of Marketing, and is also the editor of *The International Handbook of Market Research Techniques*.

ADVISORY MEMBERS

Martin Callingham was formerly Group Market Research Director at Whitbread, where he ran the Market Research department for 20 years and was a non-executive director of the company's German restaurant chain for more than 10 years. Martin has also played his part in the market research world. Apart from being on many committees of the MRS, of which he is a Fellow, he was Chairman of the Association of Users of Research Agencies (AURA), has been a council member of ESOMAR, and has presented widely, winning the David Winter Award in 2001 at the MRS Conference.

Nigel Culkin is a Fellow of The Market Research Society and member of its Professional Development Advisory Board. He has been a full member since 1982. He has been in academia since 1991 and is currently Deputy Director, Commercial Development at the University of Hertfordshire, where he is responsible for activities that develop a culture of entrepreneurism and innovation among staff and students. He is Chair of the University's, Film Industry Research Group (FiRG), supervisor to a number of research students and regular contributor to the media on the creative industries.

Professor Merlin Stone is one of the UK's most experienced consultants, lecturers and trainers in CRM, database marketing and customer service. He is a Director of WCL, specialists in change management in the public and private sectors and of Nowellstone Ltd, a recruitment, search and selection company specializing in CRM. Merlin is a visiting Professor at Bristol Business School. He has written many articles and 25 books on marketing and customer service, including *Up Close and Personal: CRM @ Work, Customer Relationship Marketing, Successful Customer Relationship Marketing, CRM in Financial Services* and *The Customer Management Scorecard*, all published by Kogan Page, and *The Definitive Guide to Direct and Interactive Marketing*, published by Financial Times-Pitman. He is a Founder Fellow of the Institute of Direct Marketing and a Fellow of the Chartered Institute of Marketing.

Paul Szwarc began his career as a market researcher at the Co-operative Wholesale Society (CWS) Ltd in Manchester in 1975. Since then he has worked at Burke Market Research (Canada), American Express Europe, IPSOS RSL, International Masters Publishers Ltd and PSI Global prior to joining the Network Research board as a director in October 2000. Over the past few years Paul has specialized on the consumer financial sector, directing multi-country projects on customer loyalty and retention, new product/service development, and employee satisfaction in the UK, European and North American markets. Paul is a full member of The Market Research Society. He has presented papers at a number of MRS and ESOMAR seminars and training courses.

Foreword

In business the critical importance of understanding, not only one's customers, but also one's own employees has finally been firmly acknowledged. Employees can be powerful ambassadors in communicating a company's values throughout the marketplace. Moreover companies want to be good corporate citizens, much of which includes ensuring they rigorously examine the employee perspective on different organizational issues and developments. Against this backdrop there was an urgent need for comprehensive authoritative, clearly written text that outlines the key principles behind undertaking professional research amongst employees.

So everyone will welcome the tremendous experience and insight Peter Goudge brings to the subject of employee research. The book provides an extremely cogent and intelligent account of the issues that need to be taken into account in making sure that one's employee research is sufficiently robust to provide a professional platform for sound organizational decision making.

I have no hesitation in commending this book to fellow market research professionals and others who regularly carry out employee research and want an update on latest techniques and developments. In addition, the book will be of great value to those undertaking employee research for the first time, including those studying for Market Research Society educational qualifications. In short, this book is an informative and invaluable read on a critically important subject.

Dr D V L Smith
Chairman, Incepta Marketing Intelligence
Professor, University of Hertfordshire Business School
Former Chairman of the Market Research Society

Acknowledgements

In the course of my career I have been fortunate to work with a huge number of people who have added to my personal development and made the time I spent as client, colleague and supplier enjoyable and rewarding. Many of these people have contributed to this book indirectly through all that I have learnt from them.

More specifically, for their direct contributions to the book, I would like to take the opportunity to thank Alex Wilke of Infocorp, Barry Fitzpatrick of Total, Charles Fair of Right Management Consultants, Kate Willis of Kate Willis Research, Lucinda Craig of Elucidation, Ray Eccles of BDI Surveys and Sam Sparrow of Cadbury Schweppes. Special thanks are due to Marilyn, for giving me the space to write the book, and to Bryony Pearce whose experience and attention to detail have been invaluable as she sought to make sense of my initial drafts.

Peter Goudge

Introduction

The sustained success of any organization is most likely to be achieved where an appropriate balance is struck between the interests of various stakeholding groups, including employees, customers, shareholders, suppliers and the wider community. To arrive at such a balance requires sound leadership and decision making at the top of the organization, and in addition, clear channels of communication so that the interests of the various groups can be represented and taken account of.

In the smallest organization or unit with just one or two people (such as a business start-up) the commonality of purpose between stakeholders is likely to be at its height, not least as far as the managers, the owners and the employees are concerned, since they will be one and the same. Yet as an organization grows there is clearly scope for a divergence of purpose between these groups. In the case of employees, when an organization grows to the point where they are numbered in tens of thousands, it is impossible to expect that everyone will share the same values or motivations, let alone (given the imperfections of any communications medium) be the possessors of identical information concerning the performance of that organization.

The art of successful management is therefore about ensuring that any divergence is minimized and the commonality of purpose is maximized. By successfully marrying communication to and from employees, the management team are more likely to have a motivated workforce that shares their vision and values, and understands what is expected of them and how they in turn will benefit. Feeling informed and knowing that their opinions and views are valued is also likely to improve employee attitudes and increase commitment to the organization. In the distillation of his work, *The Essential Drucker*, Peter Drucker (2001) succinctly sums up this fundamental task of management as making 'people capable of joint performance through common goals, common values, the right structure, and the training and development they need to perform and to respond to change'.

In turn, the benefits of having a workforce full of employees with highly favourable attitudes and commitment have been demonstrated by the WorkUSA® study (available from the Watson Wyatt website), which showed that the financial performance of such organizations is typically nearly four times better than the financial performance of companies with poor employee attitudes. Moreover, organizations with highly favourable employee attitudes have been proven to better withstand economic and other crises such as the most recent recession.

The aim of this book is therefore to demonstrate the role that market research can play in these processes of communicating with and engaging employees. As such it seeks to encourage those involved in market research to demonstrate to a wider audience the value of the techniques they have available to them. As well as offering market researchers the encouragement to become more involved in employee issues, the intention is to delineate where traditional techniques have benefits and where there are limitations. The blind assumption that things work in just the same way as they do in other areas of research is a dangerous one to make.

At the same time, it has to be recognized that there are many more people with an interest and involvement in the subject matter who will not have had the benefit of a background or training in market research. So it is hoped that this book will demonstrate the advantages of following the sound principles and practices that have been developed under the auspices of the Market Research Society.

Apart from anything else, one of the joys of being involved in employee studies is the range of issues that research can help with. The potential of this range is almost as broad as it is with consumer research. So another challenge therefore in writing this book has been to constrain the number of topics covered. Quintessentially, this is a book about involvement and participation because this is what research encourages and can facilitate. Not only can research help inform decisions about the form that participation takes, it can also act as a form of participation itself.

The starting point for the book is an examination of the major reasons for, and the benefits to be derived from, conducting research amongst employees. As with any other form of reason, the clarity of purpose with which such an exercise is framed is critical to its eventual success. In addition Chapter 1 references some of the management systems that have been developed in recent times and contributed to the growing interest in employee research.

Chapter 2 develops the theme of the inter-relationships between employees and customers, and considers the specific applications for employee research in this context. The defining requirement for most organizations is to meet the needs of their customers, and the continued success of the organization frequently depends on the interplay between employees and customers. These relationships, including the extent to which employee satisfaction is a necessary or sufficient condition of customer satisfaction, are explored in this chapter.

Chapter 3 then goes on to examine the relationships between employees and other stakeholders, notably those who own the organization. Relevant to these discussions are the efforts taken to involve employees in the ownership and management of organizations, and the growing significance of attempts to place a financial valuation on the contribution of employees. Such efforts commonly appear under the label of human capital, and some of the ways in which the valuation can be achieved are explored.

Up to this point there are frequent references to the wider subject of communications. Research and communications are inextricably linked, as they each offer mutual support to the other, while in any case research itself is a form of communication both to and from employees. Chapter 4 therefore considers the broader context of communications involving employees, highlighting the ways in which research complements other media as well as assisting with the strategic and tactical development of communications overall.

This paves the way for Chapter 5 to describe the steps that need to be taken to get the most value out of a research survey. Traditionally, employee research has relied on quantitative techniques, and it was normally in a form that lent itself to being conducted online. Since online research methods have opened up many new opportunities but also need to be used appropriately, Chapter 6 is specifically devoted to them, highlighting when other approaches still represent a better option.

Less commonly used in the past, qualitative research offers tremendous advantages to organizations in gaining a better understanding of the attitudes and motivations of their employees. Chapter 7 therefore discusses how qualitative research can be deployed to advantage, along with the particular considerations attached to conducting it among employees.

The final chapter then takes the thinking further by looking beyond the conduct of research studies to a development that mirrors the consumer 'insight' movement. This advocates closer cooperation between the owners of the different data sources covering employees, and the integration of outputs from employee research.

Following this chapter, Appendix 1 discusses the Information and Consultation Regulations, given the relevance of some of the issues covered by this EU legislation.

1 Conducting employee research: reasons and benefits

INTRODUCTION

The starting point for the book is an overview of the reasons for gathering information from employees and the benefits of so doing. There is clearly a wide range of reasons why an organization would wish to conduct employee research, so this chapter can only outline the most common. Indeed, the coverage is not exhaustive nor are the reasons mutually exclusive, while different organizations will seek to combine them in different ways. The critical requirement is to be quite clear why the exercise is being undertaken at all and what will happen as a consequence of it.

In addition, the foundations are laid for subsequent chapters which set out the principal ways in which the research will be conducted. The alternative approaches, plus any other prerequisites for an effective study, can best be examined against the backdrop of why the research is happening at all.

The overview starts with the sort of feedback-gathering exercise that has now become quite common in organizations and often goes under the heading of an employee attitude or opinion survey. Frequently these studies are based around lists of statements with which respondents are required to register their strength of agreement. The coverage of such surveys and the ways in which the findings are applied have evolved over time, so they are now likely to be as concerned with the linkages to business performance as with simply measuring employee satisfaction.

The evolution of this more traditional form of survey has reflected the increasing complexity and pace of change in corporate life. At the same time therefore there has been an expanding breadth and depth in the reasons for conducting research. The broader remit is evidenced in the growing involvement of employees in decision making and the management of change, for example when mergers or acquisitions are taking place. Meanwhile, employee research has deepened as it has become more important, for instance, to consider cultural issues and to study new priorities that have emerged such as the work/life balance.

In parallel with these developments, organizations have been seeking to benefit from various management systems and frameworks that have become available. A number of these, such as the balanced business scorecard, are examined in the final section in this chapter since the focus they have on employees as stakeholders has underwritten the importance of conducting research amongst employees.

STATE OF THE NATION

Historically, employee attitude surveys have been used as a management planning tool since they came to prominence in the early 1960s. These studies have sought to provide organizations with information about some of the fundamental people issues at a given time. The drive to obtain an understanding of employees' attitudes will typically emanate from those responsible for people management in the personnel or HR functions. Inevitably therefore the common issues covered by such studies include working conditions, reward and recognition, training and development, and other human resource policy areas.

Perhaps the most common questions to be found in such surveys are concerned with job satisfaction, or happiness with the employing organization. Some organizations seek to take a measure of morale or pride in the organization, but almost all ask something along the lines of 'How satisfied would you say you are with your current job?' Employees are then invited typically to indicate whether they are very satisfied, fairly satisfied, neutral, fairly dissatisfied or very dissatisfied. Other common areas of questioning include attitudes towards the management and leadership of the organization as well as the effectiveness of internal communication.

Inevitably, within the confines of any type of research, taking the temperature on such a wide range of topics means that there is limited scope to investigate any one in depth. Yet, for some companies, these surveys represent their only formalized and direct means of evaluating employee opinion and feedback. As such the results will enable broad areas of strength and weakness to be identified so as to assist with strategic development in any of the areas listed, as well as communication generally.

PRIORITIZING MANAGEMENT ACTION

As well as recording employee opinion on specific issues, surveys can be used to target and prioritize matters that require management action by determining those that employees regard as being in need of most urgent management action. By collecting data from a large number of individuals it is possible to generate results that are robust and enable decisions to be made with confidence, knowing that they represent the views of a good cross-section of the workforce.

Apart from giving a summary snapshot of how people feel about working in the organization, the sort of data gathered in employee surveys can be analysed in a way that identifies those factors that have the greatest impact on core employee measures, such as satisfaction, motivation or commitment. Without asking directly what is most important to employees (some of whom may have difficulty in prioritizing contributory factors in any case), an analysis can be performed to see which of the other variables or parameters in the survey influence or drive the particular measure. Hence the approach is known as key driver analysis. It is discussed at more length in Chapter 8. Having identified these key parameters the organization can then seek to align its offering to employees.

Another example of an analysis that can be performed comes from the paper given by Sheldon *et al* to the 1996 MRS Conference, which was concerned with the use of the stated preference technique. In common with many other organizations, London Underground used this approach to optimize the allocation of scarce resources in their investment decisions, taking into account customer preferences. It was therefore within this context that they decided to take a similar approach to staff investment and remuneration issues. They wished in particular to evaluate the relative monetary values that their staff placed on components of the total remuneration package (including working hours, clothing, and travel allowance).

The technique requires respondents to choose between a series of options, presented in pairs, with each option typically describing a package of features. Repeated choices are based on a statistical design so that the data analysis can derive the relative importance and potentially the monetary value of various features.

MANAGING RESPONSE TO CHANGE

Since employee research first became common, increasing competitive pressures have resulted in volatile and challenging times for the working population. Successful change management has become an essential prerequisite for survival in a rapidly evolving marketplace. In turn, understanding employees' responses to change has been increasingly recognized as essential to managing change effectively. Research is of particular value in gauging people's reaction (and the extent of any resistance) to the many changes affecting the workplace, such as the impact of new technologies, business process re-engineering and downsizing.

Then again there are the changes brought about by strategic alignments and acquisitions or mergers. Such developments can take many forms, and may involve companies that do similar things joining forces, or the combining of organizations that operate at different points in the supply chain (in the jargon, either horizontal or vertical integration). In addition, organizations may seek to join forces while retaining their separate entities or creating a new one. Depending upon the strategy it is evident that some of these situations can have a greater impact on the workforce (for example, horizontal integration of similar companies and the creation of one entity where there once had been two or more).

However, if not handled well, any of these situations can lead to the real possibility of the workforce deciding to withdraw their labour or even to leave, if they do not feel engaged by the strategy or have not been adequately informed of the intentions. It is also the case that clashes of cultures occur when organizations are joined together, and all too frequently anticipated synergies are not realized. By ascertaining from employees what their understanding is of, and how they perceive, developments as they unfold, it is possible to manage the situation and retain the involvement and commitment of employees through the process.

CASE STUDY

On either side of the millennium Total merged with first PetroFina and then Elf Aquitaine to become TotalFinaElf, before the company was renamed as Total in 2003. Inevitably, the mergers brought together different cultures and management styles, and led to a substantial number of redundancies as functions were combined.

Total UK, the marketing and distribution arm in the UK, realized the importance of giving (and being seen to give) all staff in the

---

merged company the opportunity to have their say, and therefore instituted a company-wide survey of staff attitudes. The success of the initial exercise led to it being repeated annually, and its development offers a number of pointers for the successful conduct of such surveys.

Although there had been some suspicion about how confidential the survey might be, repeated reassurance on this aspect, and the fact that it was being handled by a specialist research company, overcame the problem. Indeed, through the use of a qualitative stage of research prior to the main study, employees had been able to contribute many of the questions that were being asked, giving them a strong perception of ownership. Moreover, by reporting back with the results and action plans employees were able to readily appreciate that their views were being listened to.

With successive surveys the involvement of employees at a more local, functional, level increased as results were reported, discussed and incorporated into planning at all levels, not just the overall company level. Another achievement that was implicit in this outcome was the acceptance that the results were undeniably true; whether they were liked or not, it had to be recognized that they were an accurate reflection of how people felt, and not something to be shrugged off and ignored.

Over time the ambition of the survey has increased as it has become an integral part of the company's communication activities and has contributed to the unification of the legacy companies. As the new entity moved away from the early, pragmatic, cost considerations through to the creation of a new identity with a set of employee-oriented (and generated) values, there was also a desire to compare performance with other companies. Total opted for the benchmarking capability available from the *Sunday Times* 100 Best Companies to Work For Awards, recognizing that some loss in comparability of their own questions over time would be matched by the benefits of being able to make external comparisons.

Importantly the development of the survey has also assisted in the development of managerial skills, as local management were made aware of issues that needed to be dealt with and benefited from the participation of their teams in resolving those issues. Its success has also helped persuade the Group to do something on a global scale, while the only downside is that interest in doing additional surveys at departmental and functional levels has had

> to be checked for fear of employees spending all of their time completing questionnaires.

Other developments or plans that can benefit from seeking the views of employees, and which are increasingly evident in corporate life, are concerned with rebranding and/or repositioning. In an article about the law firm Ashurst Morris Crisp (*Daily Telegraph* London, 1 April 2004), Stefan Stern described how the company had consulted with their staff over an 18-month period on what the firm's core values were perceived to be. This enabled them to fine-tune a new brand identity that reflected the views of the people who worked in the firm, and they did so in a way that was iterative and incremental, allowing a broad consensus to develop.

In addition to proactively evaluating likely reactions to new developments, and so helping to shape how change can best be managed and communicated, employee research can also provide a useful tool for monitoring how effectively change has been implemented.

CULTURE MAPPING

Mentioned in passing above, and cutting across many of the issues in this book, is the subject of culture change. With countless books and articles taking a cultural perspective on management and organizational change, some companies have begun to take a broader view of attitudinal research, switching their attention to the group values and belief systems that underlie prevailing patterns of thought and behaviour.

Culture mapping (or profiling) seeks to identify, and then measure, the key cultural parameters within an organization. This form of research provides managers with a more objective answer to questions such as, What kind of culture do we have now? What kind of culture do we want? How successful have we been in shaping the culture of the organization? Where are the gaps between where the culture currently is and where we need it to be? It is therefore the sort of topic that warrants both a qualitative as well as a quantitative dimension to any research.

In one sense, attempting to define the culture of an organization is like searching for its DNA, except that the process is less exact and more of an art form than the approach used by scientists. Indeed, culture is not something that is static; it is dynamic and unpredictable, and so an audit must be recognized as being a helpful snapshot rather than as a definitive statement.

Culture is an amalgam of many aspects including the personal beliefs of individuals, the moral and ethical codes of the organization, and the behavioural norms and the rituals that take place. These are manifest in the language and jargon of the organization; the style and design of its premises; the reward systems; the extent to which there is an ethos of team working and the way in which decisions are arrived at; how open communication is, whether information is generally shared and the extent to which employees are encouraged to develop themselves; the acceptability of staff turnover and the type of people recruited; and whether the primary focus of the organization is on external stakeholders rather than internal processes. While some of these manifestations can be observed, many of them lend themselves to being measured through survey research techniques.

WORK/LIFE BALANCE, HARASSMENT AND STRESS

Outside of changes driven by commercial pressures, there are a number of issues now regularly included in employee surveys that reflect changes in society more generally. Attitudes to work itself change, and with such change come new norms and expectations. Hence work/life balance is a topic that is more regularly addressed, as is harassment, whether in relation to gender, religion, disability or ethnicity.

Indeed, by collecting under a general heading of demographic information such details as gender, religion, disability and ethnic origin, research surveys can be the best source of data about the diversity in the workforce that an organization has. Such data collection carries with it great responsibilities, since if the survey gives too detailed a picture of respondents, they could be identified from their answers, destroying any notion of anonymity. A balance has therefore to be struck between gathering enough detail to assist with any analysis and interpretation, and not asking for so much that anonymity could be compromised.

Increasingly stress, defined as 'the adverse reaction people have to excessive pressure or other types of demand placed on them', is becoming a factor that has to be dealt with, whatever its cause. According to research conducted by the Health and Safety Executive (HSE) in the UK, and to be found on their website, it is estimated that up to 5 million people in the UK (about one in five of the total workforce) feel 'very' or 'extremely' stressed by their work; while work-related stress costs society about £3.7 billion every year.

Stress is something that can have a multitude of origins, be very subjective in the way in which it is experienced, and not necessarily be caused by any factors under the control of the employer. However, since it will impact on the capacity of an individual to work, there are clear benefits to be gained from understanding it and dealing with the causes. Indeed, the HSE has established six standards designed with a view to improving performance through better management of contributory factors.

These standards are concerned with the demands placed on employees; the understanding of their role and responsibilities; the amount of control they have over the way they do their work; the information and support they receive from their colleagues and superiors; and the quality of working relationships (that is, the absence of unacceptable behaviours such as bullying). The final standard emphasizes the need for employees to be engaged frequently when the organization is undergoing any organizational change.

CASE STUDY

For a major UK retailer, stress (as observed in terms of absenteeism and sickness levels) was becoming an increasingly major challenge for the business. With the assistance of Right Management Consultants, it therefore sought to link employee attitude survey data generated in response to statements such as 'Stress of work is affecting me in my job performance' with sickness and absenteeism data as recorded by the HR information system, across 500 stores.

The subsequent analysis showed, possibly not too surprisingly, that stores that had a high score on such questions tended to be those with the highest sickness and absence levels. However when the analysis was taken further it was found that there was a strong correlation with some of the issues identified in the above standards, such as the performance of line management and the support provided, along with the extent of workloads.

Furthermore, an examination of the customer satisfaction measures by store (gained through a mystery shopping exercise) revealed that those stores with poorer customer satisfaction tended to be those with relatively high levels of sickness. This then made it possible to estimate the cost savings that could potentially be achieved by lowering the high level of sickness and absence observed in certain stores to a more typical level. The stores were grouped into three approximately equal-sized groups depending on their levels of absence and sickness.

The stores with the highest levels of sickness and absence had a gross profit margin that was, on average, 0.5 per cent lower than stores with average sickness and absence levels. In fact the difference in contribution between the 'high absence' and 'medium absence' groups was £30,000 per year per store. A potential cost saving of over £5 million was therefore achievable if sickness and absence levels in all 170 stores in the 'high absence' group could be managed downwards to the level of the 'medium absence' group.

Having aimed to reduce absenteeism and poor customer satisfaction by addressing stress levels, the company was in a position to do so by identifying and amending the contributory factors.

BENCHMARKING

When an organization first undertakes an employee survey there is understandably a desire to know how the results compare with other organizations. Without such a benchmark or prior experience of running such surveys it can be difficult to interpret the data. Is the figure of 60 per cent of employees agreeing with a statement good or bad?

Clearly if the usual result elicited by other organizations from a specific question is around 30 per cent (and the statement has been positively worded), then agreement at the 60 per cent level is indeed welcome, and probably suggests that this is not a cause for concern. Alternatively, if results are normally seen at around 90 per cent, then the organization is likely to make this an issue to be addressed promptly.

In order to give confidence in such comparisons, there are a number of basics that need to be in place. The most obvious is that the same question has to be posed to employees in all of the different organizations. While this does not sound hugely onerous, by setting out with the intention of comparing results with other organizations it is possible to lose sight of the issues that are pertinent to the organization itself and its employees. So care has to be exercised that the agenda is not determined solely by other organizations, as it could simply mean that the wrong questions are being asked, and the comparative data is therefore obtained, but irrelevant.

In addition to asking the same questions to ensure the validity of any comparative results, it is also necessary to check that they have been asked in the same way. Differences in methodology can affect how an individual responds to a question, most obviously when the difference is between a questionnaire that is administered by an interviewer and one that is completed by respondents themselves. Note that there could also be a margin of error attached to the results if only a sample of employees is invited to take part, as opposed to a census of all employees.

A further consideration here is whether the questions have been asked in the same sequence. The 'order effect', as it is known in market research, can have a very significant impact on the way in which the same question is answered. Perhaps one of the best examples of this comes from the popular television series *Yes, Minister*. The Permanent Secretary Sir Humphrey Appleby takes the Principal Private Secretary Bernard Woolley through two lines of questioning, both of which end with the question 'Would you oppose the reintroduction of National Service?' (National Service was effectively conscription into the armed forces for a specified period of time.)

In one sequence the questioning starts with the respondent being invited to say whether he is worried about the number of young people without jobs, before going on to discuss crime and the need for discipline amongst young people. The second sequence begins with a question about the dangers of war, and then covers the growth of armaments and the dilemma of giving young people guns and teaching them how to kill. Inevitably this sequence elicits a different response to the final question!

A further point that needs to be emphasized about external benchmarking data is the importance of knowing which organizations, or at least types of organization, make up the benchmark, and the timing of the surveys that contributed to it. Otherwise it may be possible that the benchmark data comes from organizations in completely different sectors, or that the other surveys took place some time ago and in different circumstances.

It is sometimes overlooked that a very powerful source of benchmarking data can be found within the organization itself, especially if it is made up of a group of companies. Even a stand-alone organization is likely to have a structure involving regions or functions or divisions, which facilitates comparisons. By ensuring that each part of the organization is asked the same questions at the same time it will be able to identify best practice, which can then be shared across the organization.

KEY PERFORMANCE INDICATORS

As part of the process of making broad comparisons across different parts of an organization, it has become increasingly common for companies to combine a range of scores from the employee survey into a single summary indicator (often called the employee satisfaction index). This approach also makes it easier to analyse the relationship between employee opinion/satisfaction and other indicators used to measure the performance of the organization.

Part of the impetus to present data in this way has come from the growth in the use of balanced business scorecards, which are discussed more fully later in the chapter. Meanwhile, a good example of the way in which survey results have been used in the performance management process was presented to the 1999 MRS Conference by McClymont and Briggs. They reported on the development of an employee attitude survey at Sainsbury's. From its inception in 1996 to the time of their paper, the survey had evolved from providing a voice for employees to becoming an established part of the company culture itself.

McClymont and Briggs were able to demonstrate that the survey had been used to drive change programmes as well as providing input to performance management systems. These systems provided for managers to have targets which were set and reviewed on a regular basis. These targets reflected the overall business strategy, and ensured that there was a clear and consistent framework for the business to move forward. The survey provided the people measures, and so ensured that managers took full account of the people dimension alongside all of the other parameters that they were being assessed on.

When employee surveys are used in setting management targets and monitoring performance, employee research is placed at the heart of business performance measurement, especially if the further step is taken of linking results to managerial bonus schemes. However, caution is required in using such surveys as a tool for examining individual levels of competence, or rewarding line managers when those results are based on the views of their teams. Quite simply, such surveys could be open to abuse or interference in the process, as managers exert undue influence (either positively by being 'nice' in the survey period or negatively by bullying employees).

As with any such scheme, care has to be exercised that those behaviours that can be measured (and hence targeted) are the correct ones. Targets can certainly force a change in behaviour, but it must not be at the risk of an adverse effect on other desirable behaviours.

BALANCING TOP-DOWN COMMUNICATIONS

The very process of undertaking an employee survey is itself part of a wider exchange of information between management and staff. It is therefore more than just a vehicle for extracting information from employees, and as such employee research performs a valuable role in helping to complement the top-down flow of communication within an organization.

If correctly managed, employee research can help to demonstrate that senior managers regard employees as having an important contribution to make to the planning process, and are concerned about tackling the issues they raise. In addition, surveys can provide a further mechanism for generating ideas and suggestions.

WIDENING THE IDEAS POOL

One of the other means of upward communication is a suggestion scheme. For such a scheme to be successful there must be in place an efficient and continuous process for handling the volume of suggestions and deciding on those that merit implementation. The use of an employee survey offers an alternative approach, by ensuring that good ideas are invited and fed back to decision makers at the centre of an organization.

As part of the information yield from a survey, the suggestions and ideas can be separated out and dealt with in a one-off examination by the management team, who can decide which to support and bring to fruition. When great emphasis is placed on innovation and continuous improvement, it is surprising how often companies overlook the opportunity employee research offers to tap into the knowledge and experience that exists at all levels in an organization, especially those employees who are directly customer-facing.

Such benefits become even more evident in the use of the full range of research techniques, such as focus groups and 'team listening' sessions, which are also valuable in promoting the role that staff can play in tackling problems and identifying opportunities for improvement.

In addition to providing a conduit for positive suggestions, surveys can play an equally important role in innovation by identifying problem areas. In his article 'Why workers across the EU are simply giving up' (*Daily Telegraph* London, 7 October 2004), Brian Bloch cited the example of a large German manufacturing company. Having experienced falling productivity and profitability, the company brought in consultants and imposed a series of draconian controls. Unfortunately the introduction of these controls simply exacerbated the problem and led to a spate of resignations. It was only when the top-down style of management was recognized as causing the problem, and replaced by a more open dialogue with employees, that more effective controls were introduced, leading in turn to a rise in profits. Had regular employee communication been in place beforehand, there would have been an early warning system that would have more readily identified the problem, along with a solution.

INTERNAL COMMUNICATIONS AUDITS

In looking more generally at the overall pattern of communications within an organization, employee research can also provide a useful means of assessing the relative effectiveness of each element within the communications mix. Organizations usually communicate through many different channels (face to face, telephone, e-mail, intranet, video, company magazine and so on). Evaluating how employees use these media, and which they prefer to use for different types of information, provides a vital foundation for effective and cost-efficient management of internal communications, including testing perceptions of management messages, the communication style and feedback mechanisms.

Subsequently, once it has been decided which media should be deployed to communicate specific messages, research offers the opportunity to harness the views of employees regarding specific executions and treatments, much in the same way that customer research is an important building block in the development of external communications. The importance of this subject matter is such that it is explored in more detail in Chapter 4.

EXTERNAL COMMUNICATIONS

Similarly, in a theme that is also developed later in the book, advertising aimed at external audiences regularly receives inputs from employees at both the strategic development and the executional stages of a campaign. With the development of the stakeholder philosophy, such an approach is equally applicable in areas other than direct communication with customers through advertising. One of the earliest examples used to illustrate the wider benefits of such an approach was reported by Bob Worcester in his paper to the MRS Conference in 1973.

In his paper Worcester referred to various case studies pertaining to organizations that were using employee research in conjunction with an examination of how they were perceived externally. These case studies often focused on those categories of employees (such as salespeople) who worked directly with customers or other stakeholders. One particular case study referenced was groundbreaking in its subject matter as well as its scope: the employees of Standard Oil (subsequently to become Exxon) were asked about their employer's effectiveness at controlling pollution.

The study, which was conducted in 1972 by Opinion Research Corporation of Princeton, asked employees about the company's commitment in this area as well as the effectiveness of its communications. Although many employees considered the company to be highly committed to environmental conservation and viewed the information it provided as being very credible, they nevertheless felt that both internal and external audiences were poorly informed about its pollution-related activities. The findings prompted developments in both internal and external communications, notably in focusing on what the company was actually doing in this area, as well as providing inputs to the entire conservation programme.

SUCCESSFUL RECRUITMENT AND RETENTION

Looking further out, employee research need not be restricted to current employees. Many companies use research to understand the perceptions and attitudes of potential employees. At a time when the market for skilled staff is becoming increasingly competitive, and the terms 'employer of choice' and 'the war for talent' are becoming increasingly widespread, the additional insight that this research provides can be crucial in determining the success of recruitment initiatives.

In addition to evaluating the opinions of potential recruits, research can also provide valuable insight into the reasons that staff leave a company. Exit interviews conducted by the HR department or independent agencies can be used to assess the 'push' and 'pull' factors governing staff turnover, enabling companies to respond accordingly. Indeed, within an employee survey questions concerned with intentions to remain with or to leave the organization can be very powerful business indicators for management.

CUSTOMER AND BUSINESS ALIGNMENT

As is discussed in more detail in the next chapter, many companies conduct both customer satisfaction surveys and employee attitude surveys. By coordinating these two activities it is possible to determine how staff satisfaction, motivation and commitment affect customer satisfaction and therefore business performance. In more immediate terms, they can be used to identify gaps that exist between staff perceptions of the service they deliver and customer perceptions of the service they receive, enabling companies to prioritize (and demonstrate to staff) the aspects of service that most require improvement.

In addition to the service delivery issues, employees potentially have a significant contribution (which is normally beneficial, but can be detrimental if not managed well) to make to the process of product development. In the *Financial Times* (22 October 2001) Chan Kim and Renee Mauborgne of Insead noted the role played by employees, in this instance the sales force, in the failure of a product launch by Burmah Castrol.

The company had devised an innovative system for water coolants used in metalworking industries. Previously customers would have had to choose between several hundred types of complex coolants, involving testing options on production machines. The expert system developed by Burmah Castrol was therefore able to save time, effort and expense all round by synthesizing the collective knowledge and expertise in the company. Not only did customers stand to gain from a greatly diminished failure rate, they also were being saved money.

Unfortunately the sales force, who had not been involved in the development process, viewed the system with some suspicion, as it effectively removed what they considered to be a major source of job satisfaction (derived from their role in fine-tuning the coolant that the customer ended up purchasing). They therefore felt threatened, opted to work against the system, and sales did not take off.

The lack of perceived fairness and involvement consequently wrecked a product which otherwise appeared to offer substantial benefits to the company and its customers. If the workforce had been consulted and their concerns addressed this failure could have been averted, and the company could have had a hugely successful product launch.

BUSINESS MODELS AND QUALITY SYSTEMS

Part of the imperative to look at the full range of stakeholders has come from the integrated nature of many business models and quality systems now being used by organizations. Given the importance of these models and systems to the interest in and growth of employee research, it is worth examining four leading examples in more detail. Interestingly, they were all developed in the period around 1990.

Investors in People

Investors in People (IiP) is a national quality standard developed in the UK which sets a level of good practice for improving an organization's performance through the training and development of its people.

The standard was originally based on the four principles of commitment, planning, action and evaluation. As such it represents a planned approach to setting and communicating business objectives and developing people to meet these objectives. The result is a framework for matching what people can do, and are motivated to do, with what the organization needs them to do. By ensuring that such activity is repeated on a cyclical basis a culture of continuous improvement should be engendered.

Given the need to provide evidence for the assessment, along with the principle of evaluation, IiP has contributed to the growing awareness of the need to obtain direct feedback from employees.

European Foundation for Quality Management (EFQM) Excellence Model

In the same way as the Baldridge National Quality Awards in the United States recognize the successful implementation of total quality management (TQM) principles, the EFQM introduced the Excellence Model as the framework for assessing applications for the European Quality Award. Since then it has been widely used as a management system, notably assisting organizations by providing them with a framework that allows them to undertake self-assessment. As a consequence they can understand any gaps in performance, then identify and implement solutions.

The model is based on nine criteria, which can be divided into five 'enablers' (what an organization does) and four 'results' (what an organization achieves). 'Results' are caused by 'enablers', and feedback from 'results' helps to improve 'enablers'.

The model can be summarized in the statement that 'Excellent results with respect to performance, customers, people and society are achieved through leadership driving policy and strategy, that is delivered through people, partnerships and resources, and processes.'

As with IiP there is strong encouragement to gather direct feedback from employees, pertinently in the people results area. This area is in turn divided into two subsets of perception measures (of particular relevance here since they include evidence relating to motivation and satisfaction) and performance indicators (the internal ones used by the organization to monitor, understand, predict and improve the performance of the organization's people and to predict their perceptions).

CASE STUDY

The advent of TQM provided a boost to employee communications generally as well as research specifically. One early case study that demonstrated this was provided by Ruth McNeil in 'Staff research and total quality management – looking in the mirror', a paper presented to the 1993 ESOMAR Congress. The case study concerned UML, then a subsidiary of Unilever, supplying water services to other group companies in the north-west of England.

As part of the introduction of the TQM philosophy, the company wished to explore how people felt about the company, their desire for change, and most importantly how they might contribute to this process. Research was conducted in two stages. The first was qualitative in nature, and encouraged those involved to put themselves in the position of senior managers so that they could think about how they would change the company.

This was followed by a quantitative stage which enabled all 200 employees to participate. The end product of the research was a raft of initiatives concerned primarily with improving communication across the company. Managers instituted more frequent meetings, both formal and informal, to create opportunities for discussions with staff. The minutes of the executive committee were made available to all staff. Awards were granted in recognition of those who put forward suggestions or implemented new initiatives. Appraisals were introduced for all staff.

Other developments included training plans for all staff, along with such things as the creation of a social committee and improved working conditions. Two years on, the profitability of the company had improved, and it undertook another study to check on progress in the eyes of the employees and to identify further areas of improvement. This fact alone contributed to an appreciation among employees that the company was interested in their views and recognized the essential contribution they were making to its success.

Balanced business scorecard (BBS)

Devised by Kaplan and Norton at Harvard, and first reported in the *Harvard Business Review* (1992), the BBS is a management system that seeks to balance the traditional reliance on inevitably backward-looking financial measures by incorporating perspectives that are more forward looking.

There are four perspectives that make up a BBS. Firstly there is the learning and growth perspective, which is concerned with people being in a continuous learning mode through the deployment of mentors, intranets and so on, as well as training. Next is the business process perspective, which is about internal business processes, which can in turn be subdivided into mission-oriented processes and support processes. The third perspective is the Customer perspective, focusing on the customer and primarily concerned with customer satisfaction. Finally there is the financial perspective. Although the concept seeks to balance the traditional emphasis placed on this area, it clearly is not deemed to be unimportant. Rather it is seen as a perspective that needs to be balanced by the other considerations.

From the above it is clear that some of the metrics used to assess performance, particularly in respect of learning and growth, which has subsequently acquired the shorthand expression in business parlance of the 'employee perspective', feature views and opinions gathered from employees.

One of the additional benefits for a business that seeks to integrate the relevant information sources in this way is that it facilitates a deeper understanding of, say, the linkages between employees and customers. All too often data concerning different audiences is the responsibility of different functional areas.

By way of an example, if HR is the commissioning agent for an employee survey, Marketing is likely to be responsible for a customer satisfaction study. Without the imperative to integrate the results, these surveys are very likely to be undertaken at different times and involve sampling points that are not comparable. Even if all employees take part in a survey, the customer base of most organizations is such that only a sample will be approached, and the way in which the data is collected may not permit analysis by outlet, or be compatible in terms of geographical area, for instance. A coordinated plan for all such research therefore has the benefit of permitting much more extensive analysis to be undertaken, improving the quality of the business decisions that have to be made.

Burke/Litwin

While the excellence model above considers inputs and outputs as they relate to business performance, the model developed by Burke and Litwin in 1992 is concerned with organizational change, and examines the relationship between individual performance and that of the organization as a whole. It too divides the factors contained in it into two categories; here the categories are labelled 'transformational' and 'transactional'.

The four transitional factors are the external environment, mission and strategy, leadership, and culture. Changes in the latter three are deemed likely to be caused by direct interaction with external environmental forces, and are consequently likely to affect the organization and those who work in it fundamentally. These factors are in effect those that create the climate for change.

The remaining eight factors are the transactional ones, which are more about the day-to-day operations of the organization, and as such represent the end product of any change. The factors are structure, management practices, systems (that is, policies and procedures), work unit climate, motivation, task and individual skills, individual needs and values, and finally individual and organizational performance.

The way in which change is achieved in this second category is more likely to be by way of continuous, incremental and evolutionary improvements. Another way of characterizing the difference between the two categories of factors is to associate the transformational ones with leadership of the organization, and the transactional ones with management.

The model also specifically recognizes that each of the factors interacts with some of the others. For instance, the motivation of individuals will influence the work unit climate as well as being affected by it. It is therefore an example of a model that helps to explain how change has occurred as well as how it might occur in the future. This means that the model can be directly helpful in the specification of the content of an employee survey.

CONCLUSIONS

Collectively these approaches and models, although by no means exhaustive, emphasize that the measurement of the opinions of employees, alongside those of customers and other stakeholder groups, is crucial to the improvement of business performance. Indeed, some organizations are now linking employee opinion data directly to business data such as levels of profitability growth and talent retention.

As well as contributing to the management of change, research should be integral to the strategic development and tactical execution of communications, whether these are directed internally or externally. More specifically employee research can make a contribution by identifying how best to increase levels of staff satisfaction, motivation and proactivity.

It can generate cost savings in recruitment and training by helping to reduce staff turnover. Cost savings can also be achieved because research has facilitated more effective recruitment practices or the identification of inefficient and wasteful practices. Employee research can additionally provide early-warning signals of problems that would otherwise result in disputes and the loss of productivity.

Beyond these benefits, research should be an integral component in the development of new and profitable products and services, as well as the provision of enhanced customer service, with the attendant benefits of increased customer loyalty and sales.

2 Employees and customer satisfaction

INTRODUCTION

In terms of expenditure on market research, the amount devoted to the attitudes and behaviours of customers dwarfs that concerned with employees. Yet of all the interactions between groups of stakeholders, the one between the employees who literally embody the organization and its customers is perhaps the most critical to the organization's success. As such, there is enormous potential for employees to give input to decisions on ways in which the organization presents itself to customers. This chapter therefore goes into more detail regarding the relationships between employees and customers, what can be done to make them work, how research can help, and specifically whether employee satisfaction is a sufficient as well as a necessary condition for customer satisfaction.

It is an apparently obvious assertion that 'happy employees mean happy customers', particularly in the service sector, where often the brand or delivery point is the individual employee who interacts with the customer. Indeed, there are plenty of examples in a sector like financial services (from retail banking to insurance) of customers who maintain a relationship with an individual account manager even though that person has moved to another office in a different part of the country.

However, some people are still looking for the evidence to support the assertion. For an article on the *Quality Digest* website, 'Happy employees don't equal happy customers' (1988), H James Harrington examined the lists of organizations that appeared in *Fortune* magazine: *Fortune* 500, America's Most Admired Companies, American Customer Satisfaction Index and 100 Best Companies to Work For in America, and did not find the high levels of correlation between these lists that he anticipated. This of itself does not disprove the conventional hypothesis, but it does mean that the subject requires further examination and consideration. It is worth starting by examining the permutations of happy and unhappy employees and customers.

UNHAPPY EMPLOYEES AND UNHAPPY CUSTOMERS

There can be few people who would advocate a policy of deliberately making employees unhappy. Even before considering the impact on customers it is evident that unhappy employees represent a real cost to organizations. A report produced by the Hay Group (2001) showed that those employees who are dissatisfied with their lot at work are much more likely to exhibit withdrawal behaviours such as absenteeism as well as to resign.

In an aggregation of data covering a million employees worldwide, the authors of the report also concluded that typically a third of all employees will have left an organization within two years of joining it. Turning this into a quantification of the costs to an organization, they adjudged it to represent 10 per cent of revenues or 40 per cent of profits.

Such costs do not include an allowance for other impacts on the business, such as the effect on colleagues whose morale is lowered by the views and behaviours of those contemplating resigning, or the dangers to systems and security caused by the actions of mischievous employees who are about to leave and no longer bother about the fortunes of their erstwhile employer.

While it is not possible (and probably not desirable) to eliminate employee turnover completely, this cost quantification clearly demonstrates that a reduction in employee turnover could indirectly benefit customers, say, through lower prices. Where there is direct contact between employees and customers, less frequent changes in employee turnover should also yield benefits in terms of the improved servicing that comes from continuity of contact. Frequently the information that characterizes and sustains a relationship between a customer and an organization is information in the heads of individuals working for the organization. This information could therefore be lost to the organization should any of those individuals leave.

The Hay Group article (2001) also provided evidence that non-monetary considerations (such as the opportunity to fully utilize skills and abilities, and the desire to be part of a team that is ably led and directed by capable management) can be more motivating and encourage retention better than monetary considerations.

Disproving the hypothesis that unhappy employees mean unhappy customers might go a long way towards providing support for the virtuous circle that is represented by the positive version of the link between happy employees and happy customers. Finding the data to demonstrate the negative version is more difficult, as it would appear that such situations do not make great case studies.

It is nevertheless possible to find examples of organizations with both unhappy workers and unhappy customers. Indeed Scott Paton followed Harrington's piece by postulating in 1999 the reverse hypothesis, that unhappy customers will lead to unhappy employees unless the organization establishes systems and procedures to minimize unhappy customers. In support of this argument he cited a typical scene at an airline ticket counter where an irate customer is hurling abuse at a reservation agent, who objectively has no control over delays such as those caused by fog or mechanical failure.

Consider too the takeover battle during 2003 in the UK for the supermarket chain Safeway, which took a long time to resolve because the bids were referred to the Competition Commission in view of the consolidation that could result in this important sector. The length of time before the eventual winner, Morrisons, was able to take control and resume management of the business meant that the chain lost its way and market share, while inevitably employees suffered from the prolonged uncertainty about their own futures.

Another possibility that should be considered here is the situation caused by a problem customer and the impact upon employees. Bitner, Booms and Mohr (1994) considered certain situations based on problem customers, and discussed the notion that the customer is not always 'right' or 'king'. Recognizing this clearly has implications for those organizations that have built their strategies around this concept, if they have not also equipped their employees to deal with the minority of occasions when the customer may indeed be overly aggressive, upset other customers, seek to conduct illegal activities or in some other way pose a problem. Increasingly the evidence of this occurring can be seen in the signs (notably in retail establishments and public offices) requesting that customers do not show aggression towards employees.

Another manifestation can be seen in the extent to which the subject of abuse has become a regular item on many employee attitude surveys. Abuse of and discrimination against employees on such grounds as gender, sexual orientation, ethnic origin and religion is not limited to that from other people working for the same organization. The abuse can and does come from customers or members of the general public.

UNHAPPY EMPLOYEES AND HAPPY CUSTOMERS

In 2001 Robert Sinclair and Carrie Lavis, psychologists at the University of Alberta in Canada, reported on their study of four groups of employees building circuit boards used in electronic equipment. They found that although sad employees were not more productive in terms of their output volumes, they did make half as many mistakes as their happier counterparts; so fewer boards failed quality tests, which again must result at least in an indirect benefit to customers.

Apparently these less than happy employees channelled more energy into their work than their happier counterparts, who were deemed by the authors to use a lot of their energy and attention maintaining their cheerfulness. It seems entirely plausible that sad people may devote more energy to their work in order to distract themselves from their sad feelings, while happy workers are more likely to think of their work as something that could damage their happy mood.

This begs a question about the nature of the unhappiness felt by the employees, since the reasons clearly can be manifold and are not necessarily work-related. Unhappiness can exist for personal reasons, and can be a long-term feature of that employee's personality. As Judge, Bono and Locke (2000) reported, dissatisfaction can stem from low 'core self-evaluation' (low self-esteem, low self-efficacy, an external locus of control, and neurotic thinking). It has been shown that core self-evaluations measured during childhood can predict job satisfaction as an adult. If they are not aware of this, a sad employee's manager and colleagues might think themselves responsible for the employee's unhappiness.

Alternatively, despondency can be more of a direct consequence of changes in the workplace. This can occur because certain expectations and beliefs held by the employee are not matched by reality. Typically this relates to the expectations someone has when joining an organization or moving to a new job. Expectations are such that they can be generated independently of any promises made by the employer.

In 1960 Chris Argyris clarified this notion of expectations when talking about the psychological contract. The psychological contract (see also Chapter 8) is based upon perceived obligations, and as such is a promissory contract. In contrast to formal or implied contracts, the psychological contract is inherently perceptual, with the possibility that one party's understanding or expectations may not be shared by the other.

The concept of the psychological contract attracted much interest during the 1980s as many organizations began to move towards performance-based systems of reward and shorter-term, transactional relationships with their employees. This shift away from job security and rewards based on length of service potentially presented problems for, say, those who had already worked in an organization for many years and perceived their loyalty to it to be met by a breach of the anticipated rewards from a 'job for life'.

Underpinning a concept like the psychological contract is the factor of trust, and in particular trust in one's employer. Trust therefore plays a major part in the subjective experience that is represented by a breach in the psychological contract by an employer. As a study reported by Sandra L Robinson (1996) showed:

> the likelihood of psychological contract breach, and its negative impact, can be offset if employees' trust in their employer remains high. If restructuring and downsizing continue to be facts of organizational life, then the challenge for managers is to learn how to navigate such changes in a way that preserves employees' sense of trust. By effectively managing employees' trust, organizations may be able to avoid the negative ramifications of psychological contract breach.

Some of the elements that constitute changes in and breaches of the psychological contract reflect some of the broader social changes occurring in life, and these are clearly beyond the capacity of the organization to control. As an example, the concept of the life/work balance is one that has grown in importance in recent years. The extent to which this happened over the period between 1992 and 2001 was reported by White (2001) in a study funded by the ESRC (Economic and Social Research Council). The study showed that whereas a majority of female employees had been completely or very satisfied with their working hours in 1992, by 2001 the proportion was less than one-third (29 per cent). In the same period the change for their male counterparts was equally marked, with the percentage dropping from 35 per cent to 20 per cent.

Clearly in spite of the vast range of causes of potential unhappiness, these need to monitored and tracked to ensure that they are dealt with. This includes situations when customers may currently be happy. An interesting scenario was posited by Greenway and Southgate (1985): that morale could be eroded unnecessarily when employees do not experience the satisfaction warranted by a job well done. They were reporting on their research among employees and customers of the Trustee Savings Bank in the UK. They started out with the presumption of an ideal, whereby the level of service wanted by customers was actually the level that they received; and that employees and customers would share the same vision of what that level of service would be.

For the quantitative stage of their investigations the authors used a technique known as SIMALTO (simultaneous multi-attribute-level trade-off), and one of their major findings was that employees consistently rated their performance at a lower level than customers did. Although employees were being asked to respond in this research according to how they perceived customers' requirements and satisfaction, it does still highlight a situation in which there is the potential for a mix of happy customers and unhappy staff.

Although there are many reports of situations in which there is a strong correlation between the views of customers and employees as to what constitutes service quality, this study was neither the first nor the last to demonstrate that perceptions can vary between the two groups.

In their 1994 paper Bitner, Booms and Mohr suggested some explanations for this. They commented on the importance of roles and role expectations. In some sectors these are well defined, and hence they lead to common expectations by employees and customers. In addition, some encounters are repeated more frequently than others, reinforcing the knowledge of the 'script', or the structures that describe the way in which role behaviours occur. While sometimes sub-scripts (or the prescriptions for handling matters when something goes wrong) are not so well known, and this hinders a common appreciation of what constitutes good service, generally the more routine and frequent the occurrence (the authors cited the example of being seated in a restaurant), the greater the likelihood that employees will share the same view as customers of what constitutes good service.

The other theoretical construct that is relevant to this is attribution theory, since different people can attribute different causes to the same event, not least when individuals either wish to take credit for any success or deny responsibility for anything that went wrong. Bitner, Booms and Mohr (1994) noted that this is something that is more likely to colour the judgement of an employee than a customer. This highlights the fact that employees can be more concerned with internal processes, while customers will be focused on the outcome (whether they get what they want). Viewing the issue in this way helps to explain why employees may have difficulty in seeing matters from a customer's perspective.

HAPPY EMPLOYEES AND UNHAPPY CUSTOMERS

In response to his original article Harrington received many well-argued responses, which prompted him to develop his thoughts in a second article early in 1999. As part of his own defence, he quoted the example of a visit to a computer store, where an employee was engrossed in technical conversation with a fellow 'techie'. The conversation was prolonged, covering many topics not related to the purchase that was being made, and left the observer feeling a disgruntled (potential) customer. Yet here was an employee who was probably in his dream job, spending all day in an environment which left him extremely happy, and with huge job satisfaction.

This example from the retail sector is one that many people can probably recognize from their own empirical evidence of shop assistants who are happy in their roles and in the company of like-minded colleagues, but who perhaps are not always alert to the possibility of delighting the store's customers. Examples can clearly be found from other sectors. Harrington also recalled his time as a development engineer at IBM, where he admits that the things he wanted to work on and the things customers wanted from IBM were very different. His primary interest was in design, and he wanted to work on something he could patent, not on things that IBM could sell.

Moving on from those situations in which the intrinsic job-interest to an employee may cut across notions of service that are deemed acceptable to customers, an all-too-frequent cause of difficulties is an ill-thought-through system for targeting and possibly rewarding employees. A classic example of this is drawn from call centres, where the agents are paid according to the number of calls fielded. The superficial business logic is easily understood: that is, it is driven by a desire to eliminate waiting times on the telephone for customers. However the law of unintended consequences takes over, as can happen, and the agents make sure that they keep the length of the calls to a minimum so they can move on to the next one. Unfortunately, for many customers this means there is not enough time for their problems to be addressed, let alone solved, and it will probably result in them having to make further calls until they achieve a resolution.

HAPPY EMPLOYEES AND HAPPY CUSTOMERS

There are many examples available that seek to demonstrate this 'happy' combination and IT is a fertile area. Where employees understand what matters to customers and use this intelligence to identify the problem, they can fix it and take the necessary action to prevent it from recurring. This significantly reduces the impact of IT failure on their clients' businesses.

In 'Managing and measuring for value: the case of call centre performance', the Cranfield School of Management highlighted some notable examples of organizations adopting an approach that sought to capitalize on such intelligence. First, the European airline bmi took this approach, and reduced queues at ticket offices, check-ins and boarding gates. The airline's IT director Richard Dawson is quoted as saying: 'Over the last two years calls have been reduced by 40 per cent and time to fix by 70 per cent.'

Another instance comes from Fujitsu, the IT solutions provider, which had a self-imposed time limit on calls. When it got rid of this time limit staff were in effect given permission to fully resolve customer queries. This had the effect of reducing the number of unnecessary calls by as much as 60 per cent, and increasing customer satisfaction. Moreover, staff turnover fell sharply, from 42 per cent to 8 per cent, as staff gained more job satisfaction, while operating costs were reduced by 20 per cent.

Continuing with this theme, Joy LePree (*MSI News-Line Weekly*, 21 April 2003) reported a case involving the Naval Air Depot at Cherry Point, North Carolina. The depot struggled to meet deadlines for getting aircraft repaired and back in service. When the situation was analysed it was found that the facility's overall business philosophy of keeping a lid on costs was at the root of the problem. This was then changed so that the depot's most important business metric became throughput, or the number of aircraft repaired and returned to service in a given time period. That number doubled in a year, clearly pleasing the depot's customers. The employees and managers at the depot were also happy as they were able to improve customer service without a significant impact on their budgets. Above all else this is another demonstration of how important and interconnected the business strategy is to the happiness of employees and customers.

No less a person than Jack Welch was said to rely heavily on employee satisfaction data when he was running General Electric. In a 2001 speech before the National Association of Manufacturers, Don Wainwright, president of Wainwright Industries, winner of the Malcolm Baldridge National Quality Award, was reported by Infoquest as saying that 'Jack Welch uses only three indicators to run giant General Electric. He'll tell you that the most effective and only numbers he needs to know are, in order of importance: employee satisfaction, customer satisfaction and cash flow.'

Despite the anecdotal evidence, for many it remained unclear whether there was a causal link between employee and customer satisfaction. In 1996 Ryan *et al* warned that there was 'insufficient evidence for the popular wisdom that employee attitudes cause customer satisfaction'. They acknowledged the commonsense argument, and that some research testified to employee and customer attitudes influencing each other, but argued that this could be because one was reflective rather than predictive of the other.

LOYALTY AND COMMITMENT

An overview of this research gives rise to the conclusion that it is not enough simply to have a happy workforce, desirable as that may be, since their happiness may not necessarily be derived from anything that the company has done. Indeed it may not lead to any productive benefits for the organization, if the employees are somehow cocooned in a state of happiness and divorced from the imperatives driving that organization. Someone whose abilities are underused because there is not enough work to do may be very happy in being paid to spend company time reading books and magazines, yet clearly this is an inefficient use of resources for the organization, and with no discernible benefit to any stakeholders (with the possible exception of society as a whole, since there is one less person looking for employment).

Consequently commentators have looked for measures that go beyond satisfaction, such as loyalty. This does have the virtue of implying a connection with the organization, since the assumption is that the loyalty is exhibited towards it. However, care needs to be exercised, since there is the danger that loyalty will be confused with long service.

Service records are clearly vital pieces of information for an HR function. At an individual level they demonstrate what has been achieved, and give guidance about suitable future opportunities, not least in the important area of succession planning. At an aggregate level, there is the possibility that superficial judgements will be made about the desirability or otherwise of groups of employees remaining with the organization for a long (or short) time. If many people have been around a long time, it could militate against the need for adaptability when changes have to be made. If many people are new to the organization it could lead to a waste of resources, if the mistakes of the past are recreated without the benefit of the experience of those who have been through it before.

A stronger measure than loyalty that has been postulated is commitment. Jamieson and Richards (1996) described the application of the conversion model, as developed by Dr Jan Hofmeyr, to employees. The model has been successfully deployed in research amongst customers, where it seeks to categorize them as entrenched, average, shallow or convertible according to their commitment to and involvement with the brand under study.

As the authors point out, the model is particularly relevant to employees, since it has been shown that switching between 'brands' can occur when satisfaction is high, but does not always occur when satisfaction is low. Yet where involvement is high, conversion is delayed; and where it is low, it happens easily. Apart from satisfaction, commitment is an amalgam of involvement, inertia and interest (or lack of) in alternatives.

In their studies, Jamieson and Richards did find that long service does not necessarily denote commitment: those who have recently joined can be more committed than those who have been there longer. They also demonstrated that there is typically more commitment amongst those in senior positions, an outcome that is often in evidence from employee opinion surveys.

The authors went on to record those factors that characterized a workforce that is less committed: when they feel their contribution is not valued or appreciated; when formal communication is supplanted by the grapevine; and when they perceive the organization to be poorly managed or led.

The use of an approach like this has the additional merit of being able to contrast, and perhaps subsequently align, the perspective of customers with that of employees.

EMPLOYEE ENGAGEMENT

A variation on the theme of commitment is that of engagement. This can be characterized in terms of the understanding of and delivery against the business strategy. It therefore embraces how the organization presents itself to its customers and how it relates to its employees, and as such carries implications for the measurement of ways in which employees make a difference to the success of the organization.

In their report entitled 'The drivers of employee engagement', Robinson, Perryman and Hayday (2004) set out six characteristics of an engaged employee. These characteristics include having belief in the organization and a desire to work to make things better. In addition it is about having an understanding of the business context and the 'bigger picture' as well as keeping up to date with developments in the field. Moreover engaged employees should demonstrate a respect for, and a desire to help, colleagues along with a willingness to 'go the extra mile'.

There are similarities between some of these characteristics and the personal qualities and behaviours that contribute towards organizational citizenship, discussed later in this chapter. However, as the authors go on to point out, engagement is more of a two-way process. Indeed they define it as follows:

> A positive attitude held by the employee towards the organization and its values. An engaged employee is aware of business context, and works with colleagues to improve performance within the job for the benefit of the organization. The organization must work to develop and nurture engagement, which requires a two-way relationship between employer and employee.

In their studies the authors found, from analyses of employees in the National Health Service, that there was a correlation between engagement levels and some other factors such as age and length of service. Typically, those who were older or had been with an organization longer were likely to be less engaged, with the exception being those aged over 60, who were more engaged than anyone else. Having an accident or an injury at work or experiencing harassment (particularly if the manager is the source of the harassment) was also found to have a negative impact on engagement.

In contrast those who have a personal development plan, and who have received a formal performance appraisal within the past year, are likely to have significantly higher engagement levels than those who have not. Generally those in managerial or professional roles are also more likely to be engaged than support staff.

From this latter point there is a connection to what is driving engagement. The authors found that the paramount driver is a sense of being valued and involved. This in turn can be assisted by being given opportunities to contribute ideas and make decisions, as well as taking an interest in people as individuals and helping them develop their careers. These actions clearly place a premium on the participation of line managers in engaging employees, as it is the clearest way in which the organization can recognize the contribution and qualities of employees.

Research by Towers Perrin, reported by personneltoday.com in December 2004, put a slightly different slant on engagement. In addition to the crucial nature of showing interest in the well-being of employees and helping them with their development, the research concluded that the top five most important elements also included the need for employees to have challenging work to do and the appropriate authority to do a good job. In addition it was seen as being essential that senior managers lead by example.

This research also analysed the relationship between the engagement levels at companies and their impact on financial indicators. The conclusion was that companies with engagement levels above their industry sector's average outperform their peer group, on aggregate, by 17 per cent in terms of operating margin. However the report stops short of asserting direct causality between engagement and profitability, given the very large number of parameters involved.

Engagement is in all probability likely to vary with and be affected by different factors in different organizations. Hence, given the importance of measurement in this area, it is extremely important that any efforts to gauge and monitor engagement are undertaken on a bespoke basis, taking into account the specifics of the organization concerned.

The linkages between employee effectiveness, customer satisfaction and, ultimately, shareholder returns have become known as the employee–customer profit chain.

EMPLOYEE–CUSTOMER PROFIT CHAIN

Perhaps the most quoted example of a study that examined this relationship between employees and customers is the one concerned with Sears and written by Rucci, Kirn and Quinn in the *Harvard Business Review* (1998). The report followed a major turnaround in the fortunes of the company after a decade of decline. One of the principal components in this process was the creation of a model which incorporated the softer measures of satisfaction amongst employees and customers alongside easier-to-gather data such as revenues and profits. Although the authors acknowledge that many organizations may not have the will to collect all of the data necessary to chart the linkages from employee behaviour through customer satisfaction and on to profitability, they also make the point that doing this on its own is not sufficient. What is also needed is the willingness of managers to accept and buy in to the modelling, and the deployment of it in such a way that the employees themselves see how it works and how their own efforts impact on the success of the business.

Indeed the development of the model was in itself a demonstration of how the participation of managers and employees helps with the buy-in and subsequent usage. Task forces were formed in an effort to identify ways of achieving (and measuring) progress towards the goal of world-class status. Research surveys that had generated data from customers and staff were studied; focus groups were conducted amongst a large cross-section of employees as well as customers.

The early direction for where Sears needed to head was encapsulated in a statement of it being a 'compelling place to work, to shop and to invest'. The hard work that then had to be undertaken was the establishment of the relationships (using causal pathway modelling) between the various parameters that linked employee attitudes with those of customers, the resultant purchasing behaviours and ultimately the revenue and income growth that would reward investors. And once this was achieved the data had to be collected (across time as well as 800 stores) to verify these relationships.

The areas that were shown to have an impact on employee behaviour and hence customer satisfaction were grouped into two categories. The first was concerned with attitudes towards the job (liking the kind of work, obtaining a sense of accomplishment, being proud to say who they work for, the impact of their workload, the physical working conditions and treatment by supervisors). The other category was about the company (feeling good about the future, whether it would be able to change and compete, understanding of the business strategy and the connection between their work and the strategic objectives).

The effort taken in developing the model was rewarded by an ability to highlight how effort in one area would lead to results in another. One example quoted in the report is 'A 5 point improvement in employee attitudes will drive a 1.3 point improvement in customer satisfaction, which in turn will drive a 0.5 per cent improvement in revenue growth'.

Once the model had been tested, the challenge then was to take it out to the workforce as part of an education process which also covered broader territory, since it was discovered that there were massive misconceptions of things like the amount of profit made per dollar of revenue collected (in reality just 2 per cent against a median expectation of 45). The task ahead clearly transcended communication, and hence required a high degree of involvement, which led to the decision to conduct a cascaded series of gatherings ('town hall meetings') so that everyone could participate. The principal exercise in which everyone was expected to participate involved the use of 'learning maps' (pictures of, say, a town or store which led participants through a business process). In the process everyone was encouraged to put forward suggestions for improved performance at a local level, based on the information supplied to them. At the conclusion of the report, the authors were able to point to increased levels of employee and customer satisfaction at a time when the retail sector in general was less favourably viewed, and to the impact on revenues and market capitalization.

Another example of a successful employee–customer profit chain taken from North America comes from the Canadian Imperial Bank of Commerce (CIBC). In a paper 'Does customer satisfaction pay?' Hill discusses how the bank, which has 1,300 branches, uses an employee survey to produce a composite measure of 'employee commitment' at branch level. It also uses customer surveys to establish a measure of customer loyalty by branch. Both surveys are compared with branch profitability. The bank has learnt that a 5 per cent increase in employee commitment results in a 2 per cent gain in customer loyalty, which in turn drives a 2 per cent gain in profit. For CIBC this was worth $72 million in one year.

Hill also cites other companies that have built similar models, including Dow Chemicals, for whom a 1 per cent increase in loyalty generates a 1.2 per cent increase in account share, while IBM demonstrated that a 1 per cent increase in its Customer Satisfaction Index was worth an extra $500 million in sales over the following five years.

CASE STUDY

A recent example from the UK concerned the Nationwide Building Society which had analysed 11 years' worth of data from employee surveys along with two years' data from surveys amongst customers, totalling 1.5 million data records. The results overall showed that the longer employees had worked for the organization, the better the business performance. This performance was driven by the following factors: having pride in working for a successful organization; perceived fairness of the pay system; trust in senior management; the opportunity to develop and use skills; and recognition of good work.

In examining the analysis it was recognized that employee satisfaction of itself did not necessarily result in improved performance: the issue was rather how that was translated into employee and customer loyalty and commitment. As a consequence actions were taken specifically in respect of pay scales and the engineering of a more mature workforce, such that the average age of the 16,000 employees increased by at least one year.

The fruits of these efforts have been demonstrated in the increased size and profitability of the business (the addition of 56,000 customers, improved customer satisfaction ratings, the growth of the personal loan book and sales of general insurance).

Source: Doug Morrison, 'Happiness is the key to bigger profit', *Sunday Telegraph*, 6 March 2005.

Further evidence comes from a previous study from the UK, carried out by researchers employed by the Institute of Work Psychology at the University of Sheffield (Patterson *et al*, 1997). They also found a strong correlation between employee satisfaction, employee organizational commitment and overall business performance.

CUSTOMER RELATIONSHIPS

Earlier it was noted that financial services is one of the sectors where there is empirical evidence of the importance to customers of the relationship they enjoy with employees. Customers who appreciate the help and support given by a manager or adviser will continue to deal with that individual even if he or she is moved to another outlet or region. Their attachment to the brand of bank is not so much through the organization but through the representatives of it. Indeed, even without this strength of association, it is still common for customers to exhibit greater favour towards the local branch and those employees who work there than to the organization as a whole.

This identification with the local brand presence, and particularly the association with the employees of the organization, is something that was examined by Reynolds and Beatty (1999) with respect to retail clothing. Their study covered a range of upmarket department and specialty stores across the United States. They noted the inter-relationship of the social and functional benefits (time saving, convenience, advice, better decisions) of knowing the salesperson.

Knowing the salesperson leads to greater satisfaction with that individual and then with the company, laying the foundation for greater loyalty to the salesperson and the company and ultimately a greater share of purchasing of goods from that company. Interestingly while they found that satisfaction with the salesperson led to customers recommending that person to others, there was not necessarily the equivalent word-of-mouth benefit to the company. As Czepiel had noted in 1990, loyalty such as that exhibited to salespeople is built on trust, attachment and commitment, all of which values are more deeply exhibited in personal relationships.

It is generally accepted that loyal customers are more profitable, if for no other reason than the costs of acquiring new customers or the greater effort needed to persuade less loyal ones seriously impact upon profitability. Meanwhile Deming noted in *Out of the Crisis* (1986) that profit in business comes from repeat customers and personal recommendation. This is why some organizations do things like making questionnaires available at the point of sale in order to capture spontaneous feedback from customers about employees who have been particularly helpful.

However, when analysing the relationships customers enjoy with an organization it has to be remembered that not all customers are looking for the same sort of relationship. Indeed, the same customer can be looking for variations in the nature and intensity of that relationship at different points in time, and in many instances may not be seeking a relationship at all, but merely wishing to carry out a single transaction.

While the organization can seek to manage this relationship it cannot of course control it as, even allowing for the wishes of the customer, it can be influenced by factors that are literally out of its control such as the actions of competitors or other developments in that marketplace.

Dr John Gattorna, a recognized authority on supply chain design, postulated in a speech in 2003 that key dimensions in a relationship are whether it is loose or tight, and the extent to which demand for the goods or services in question is predictable. It also has to be borne in mind what it is that customers are actually buying. As Heskett, Sasser and Schlesinger said in *The Value Profit Chain* (1997), 'Customers don't buy quarter-inch drills; they buy quarter-inch holes.' So the key requirement is to find out what the priorities of the customers are, not just to make and maintain a better drill.

EMPLOYEES AS 'REAL' CUSTOMERS

One of the more obvious ways in which employees can be expected to truly empathize with customers is when they are themselves a customer of the organization that employs them. Sometimes this is simply not possible. By definition someone employed as a consultant or adviser in an employment bureau or social security office would not be in the position of seeking the services available to those who are currently out of work.

However, even where employees are using the products or services of their employer they are frequently doing so on a preferential basis, which limits the scope for them to understand the issues facing customers. Somebody working for a car manufacturer may be able to purchase a model at significantly less cost, and have access to better servicing and repair facilities, than if he or she was not an employee. Those working in a bank or other retail outlet are unlikely to have to queue up with other customers to pay in cheques or pay for their weekly purchase of groceries. And since queuing can be a major source of irritation for customers, it is an aspect of life that employees will not so readily appreciate.

In order to help employees with an objective representation of how customers are treated by the organization, there are research methodologies that can usefully supplement the more traditional reliance on interviews with customers recalling their experiences. A researcher who is there to record and subsequently analyse the transaction may accompany a customer. Alternatively, using an approach known as mystery shopping, a researcher will conduct a transaction personally, having been specifically briefed to record the way in which it was handled.

INTERNAL 'QUASI' CUSTOMERS

When employees are not users of the products and services of their employer, they are still very likely to be the 'internal' customer of someone else in that organization. The salesperson or the adviser will be the customer of the manufacturing arm, whether the employing organization is producing consumer goods or financial services. The strategists will be the customers of those gathering data on markets and performance. The call centre and virtually everybody else in the organization is likely to be a customer of the IT function.

In the latter years of the 20th century, an awareness of the importance of service within the organization led to the creation of what seemed like an industry that was sadly introverted and disproportionate to the effect that it had on the external customer. Farner, Luthans and Sommer (2001) commented on the quantity of descriptive, anecdotal literature on internal service, yet they had found little empirical assessment of this 'hot topic' in total quality.

They remarked that although the concept of viewing fellow workers as customers made intuitive sense, there was still a debate among both academics and practitioners as to the real value of internal customer service to the service quality to external customers. They therefore took the example of a large food and grocery wholesaler in order to make an empirical examination of the impact that internal customer service has on external customer service. Unfortunately their conclusion was that internal customer service seems to have a relationship with external customer service that is complex and at best mixed.

Meanwhile, considerable effort has been devoted to creating and monitoring service level agreements between internal functions, and even processes for the transfer of 'funds' between them to replicate the purchase of services. It therefore became something of an industry in its own right. While there is a compelling argument that every employee is a link in the chain by which the organization ultimately meets the needs of its customer, the extent to which processes are built up to sustain this argument is more debatable. At a minimum there is the danger that employees are asked for their views in research for their 'supplier' colleagues too frequently and they become progressively less inclined to take part in any further research.

In retrospect and with some organizations in particular, this may have been a necessary stage in the journey of the organization to becoming customer-oriented. It may well have been helpful to those who subscribe to the philosophy that 'it can't be managed if it can't be measured'. However, once the profile of customer orientation has been raised in this way by making it a component of everyday life, there will be less need for reinforcement through such processes.

Indeed, there is clearly much more to be considered in the context of relationships between employees than simply seeing one to be the customer of another. These broader considerations are best illustrated by reference to the concept of organizational citizenship behaviour.

ORGANIZATIONAL CITIZENSHIP BEHAVIOUR

In 1988 Organ defined organizational citizenship behaviour (OCB) as 'individual behaviour that is discretionary, not directly or explicitly recognized by the formal reward system, and that in aggregate promotes the effective functioning of the organization'. While his is not the only definition of OCB, Organ's statement of the five component behaviours that represent organizational citizenship is widely accepted. Firstly there is altruism, which is defined in this context as helping fellow employees with tasks or problems relevant to the work of that organization. Second there is conscientiousness, which involves discretionary behaviour going well beyond minimum requirements of the role. The third behaviour, civic virtue, is an indication of a willingness to participate responsibly in the life of the organization. Then comes sportsmanship, defined as any behaviour demonstrating tolerance of less than ideal circumstances without complaining. Finally there is courtesy, which includes efforts to prevent work-related problems with others.

The principal way in which such behaviours can influence organizational performance arises from the way in which they help people to work together, whether within or across groups. In turn this also frees up management and supervision time, improving effectiveness outside of the team. OCB can also influence customer satisfaction. For example, conscientious employees act beyond customer expectations, and those exhibiting civic virtue make suggestions to improve quality and customer satisfaction. In addition, sportsmanship and courtesy can create a positive climate among employees that spills over to customers.

While there is less evidence of a quantifiable impact on customers and their own behaviours (in part reflecting the construction of citizenship behaviours from an internal perspective) a study by Koys (2001) demonstrated that positive employee satisfaction, citizenship and retention in year one influenced customer satisfaction and profitability in year two. The strongest findings were that organizational citizenship behaviour influences profitability and employee satisfaction influences customer satisfaction.

In some quarters these behaviours have been further characterized in terms of a 'thinking performer': a person who is prepared to do more than is required of him or her by the job description. It is also possible to envisage the individual behaviours in a broader context, most notably in the case of civic virtue.

EMPLOYEES IN THE WIDER WORLD

Beyond the immediate role and function of an employee, individuals have the potential to represent their employer and be an ambassador for the organization on a wider stage, thereby influencing the views of customers and potential customers alike. In recent years the importance of the corporate social responsibility (CSR) of organizations has received considerable support. In the UK the government has its own website devoted to the topic: http://www.societyandbusiness.gov.uk/whatiscsr.shtml

The discussion around CSR has tended to concentrate on issues related to the environment and sustainable development goals. However, the subject is clearly much broader than this, as it is also about how business takes account of the economic and social impacts of the way it operates. In many ways it is the corporate equivalent of OCB, since it encompasses the voluntary actions taken over and above compliance with minimum legal requirements, as the organization addresses both its own competitive interests and the interests of wider society.

It therefore encompasses how the organization treats those who work for it, as well as how those employed by it represent it in a wider context outside the business premises. The former, concerned with what happens in the workplace, will see the organization judged on such facets as equality of opportunity, family-friendly policies, and reasonable remuneration for work undertaken.

In addition to these manifestations of the way the organization treats its employees, it will be assessed by the community it operates in by virtue of how it and its employees behave. This is sometimes described as a licence to operate, since it reflects the willingness of the community to accept and interact with that organization locally. The organization can support local communities through the provision of resources and/or the time and involvement of its employees. Although many employees will wish to be involved in activities that benefit the wider community, not all of them will view these activities as being done on behalf of their employer. Instead it may be something that is a personal interest to be pursued quite separately from their employment.

In the same way that an organization will seek to match the contribution of its employees to the expectations of its customers, it clearly makes sense to identify where there would be an optimal match between the expectations of the community and those activities with which employees are willing to be involved. Research can play its part in this identification process. In addition, the measurement of such involvements allows those organizations that wish to do so to benchmark their efforts against others.

The body known as Business in the Community has a corporate responsibility index (to be found on the bitc.org.uk website). This covers the management of four key areas: community, environment, marketplace and workplace. It can assist organizations by identifying gaps in performance and establishing where improvements can be made. The index also facilitates the demonstration to stakeholders that business is taking the lead in promoting awareness on public reporting, with the attendant benefits to trust in business and transparency in business performance.

CONCLUSIONS

Not everyone reports a causal link between actions designed to boost the happiness or satisfaction of employees and improvement in customer satisfaction. There are plenty of examples reporting situations of 'mutual happiness', with both employees and customers being the beneficiaries of a particular business decision.

What is clear is that policies need to be designed to provide an overall direction, and systems need to be put in place to ensure that the motivation of employees supports actions that will, and will be seen to, benefit customers and the community at large.

A central component of any policy will be communication, given the benefits of engaging the support of employees for the aims of the organization. In addition such intentions are also crucially dependent on the effectiveness of the management team, given the need to recognize the contribution of employees as part of the engagement process.

At the very least it is important to take regular readings of employee attitudes in order to gauge how they may be shifting and responding to events. Such studies can then be tailored to link in with complementary studies of customer satisfaction and expectations. These studies should be undertaken in a manner that reflects the particular circumstances of the organization and the influences upon it. While it is attractive to apply a model established in another area, this can be fraught with danger when it ignores relevant factors specific to the organization.

3 Employees, shareholders and capital

INTRODUCTION

The previous chapter considered the inter-relationships between employees and customers, and specifically the notion of the employee–customer profit chain, where the ultimate beneficiaries include the shareholders. In addition, employees are likely to be influenced by communications aimed at other audiences such as shareholders, notably in the case of annual reviews and the annual report and accounts.

It is therefore worthwhile considering the inter-relationships between employees and shareholders. Although few employees other than those in the investor relations function have direct contact with shareholders, in contrast to the employee–customer linkages which are often very direct, it is crucial that the interests of employees, customers and shareholders are balanced so as to avoid a situation where one group suffers at the expense of the others. As Reichheld pointed out in his seminal work *The Loyalty Effect* (1996), business is not a zero-sum game where investors can only make more money at the expense of customers and employees, and vice versa. Rather he proposes the concept of virtuous profit, which is the result of creating value, sharing it, and building the assets of the business.

In many instances an individual can be an employee, customer and shareholder of the same organization, but this chapter concentrates on the links between employees and shareholders. It examines the benefits of being, as well as the encouragement to become, a shareholder.

In addition, the notion of people as capital is explored. For many years labour and capital were considered quite separately in any discussion of economic theory related to the factors of production. Yet increasingly the premium attached to knowledge and innovation has led to terms such as intellectual capital and human capital featuring in business, suggesting that the distinction has blurred. Indeed, increasing efforts have been made to place a financial valuation on the contribution made by employees, with such valuations being informed by research studies concerned with the attitudes and behaviours of employees. Moreover, such developments have specifically led in the UK to demands for organizations to include a commentary on human capital in their operating and financial reviews.

HAPPY EMPLOYEES AND HAPPY SHAREHOLDERS

It is not the intention to go to the full extent of considering the permutations of happy and unhappy employees and shareholders, as was done for customers in the previous chapter. Indeed, formal research conducted among shareholders is still relatively uncommon. Nevertheless, it is still worth examining the evidence that supports a positive correlation between the happiness of the two groups, with the happiness of shareholders or stockholders taken to be indicated by the increased valuation of a company's stocks and shares.

In a variation of the analysis performed by Harrington (1998, 1999), Robert Levering of the Frank Russell Company presented some results in April 2004 which showed the superior investment performance of *Fortune* magazine's '100 Best Companies to Work for in America'. Between 1997 and 2003, the stock of the companies identified in this list outperformed the Standard and Poor's 500 by over 430 per cent.

The winningworkplaces.org website on which this study appears also highlights a worldwide study by Watson Wyatt in 2001, which showed the value of employee-friendly companies' stock increased by 64 per cent over five years compared with an increase of only 21 per cent for stock prices of companies with the least employee-friendly workplaces. Previously Heskett, Sasser and Schlesinger had shown, in their 1997 analysis over a 10-year period, that the stock price of companies that made substantial investments in employee loyalty and satisfaction increased by over 147 per cent, almost double the increase in stock prices of their nearest competitor.

Perhaps one of the companies most associated with the linkages between employees and shareholders is Southwest Airlines. Gittell's study (published in 2003 following eight years of research) found that the airline, known for its progressive and innovative people practices, had the highest profitability of any US carrier, had a total market value that exceeded that of all other US airlines combined, and had the highest employee productivity of any major US carrier.

The potential for the most direct link between employees and shareholders is created by the granting of shares to employees. As Baker and Tilly have found in their studies of the alternative investment market (AIM) in the UK, companies that wish to expand through a flotation are able to motivate their employees by allowing them to become shareholders. In the case of established companies there are several routes by which employees can become shareholders.

Detractors of share ownership by employees may point to companies such as Enron, where employees were strongly encouraged to invest large amounts of their savings in company stock, ultimately to a disastrous effect on their prosperity when the shares collapsed. In this instance there was also the knock-on effect of seeing 401K retirement plans take a hit, as Enron had matched individual contributions to them using company stock.

However, this example says more about the leadership and governance of the organization than anything inherently wrong with encouraging employees to share in the successes (and failures) of the company. Open and honest communication about the way in which the business was operating and what the future held for it would have enabled employees to make better informed decisions about how and where their savings should be invested.

COMPLETE CONVERGENCE

It would be very rare for the shares in a publicly quoted company to be held exclusively by the employees, and it would be even rarer for the shares to be distributed across all the employees. The complete convergence of the interests of owners and employees is more likely to be found in a private company. Yet in many ways this can be seen to also represent the convergence of quite different ideologies, as at the extreme it becomes indistinguishable from the notion of a cooperative movement.

Cooperatives flourished in Victorian times, taking many forms, and some survive today. Some protect the interests of members or contributors, such as building societies and other mutual organizations in the financial sector. Others are formed to provide benefits to consumers, such as the Co-operative Wholesale Society and Co-operative Retail Services.

The idea with these was that the benefit accrued to members through the payment of a dividend proportionate to the amount spent by a member. In practice the distribution tends to be limited by the need to retain reserves to support the development of the business.

A workers' or producers' cooperative is run for the benefit of those who work in it. An excellent example comes from Spain, where the Mondragon Corporacion Cooperativa (MCC) was set up in 1956 by five young engineers to make paraffin cooking stoves. It has since grown to be one of the largest companies in Spain with over 70,000 members, and although not all of them are now member-owners, the main focus of the MCC still remains the creation of owner-employee jobs. Statistics from their website show the Mondragon cooperatives to be twice as profitable as the average corporation in Spain, with employee productivity surpassing any other Spanish organization. The organization is focused on social success, involvement of the people and industrial democracy.

Interestingly the idea of a workers' cooperative is firmly identified with the political left, while the support for wider share ownership has tended to be associated with the political right. Yet ultimately where share ownership is primarily in the hands of employees the net effect is the same, with the employees exercising control over the organization.

The only potential difference between a workers' cooperative and a company owned by its employees through shares is that a cooperative is likely to be run on a basis of 'one member one vote', whereas voting rights determined by shareholdings will take account of the relative size of those shareholdings. Being owned by the employees is not the whole story, since the governance of any such organization may preclude the full participation of employees. This is why the success of John Lewis (see the box) is testimony to the constitution that established the partnership over 75 years ago.

A partnership is another form of organization that can be said to have its employees as the owners (provided that ownership is not concentrated in the hands of a very small minority of the individuals working in it). The John Lewis Partnership, the retailer and the UK's largest unquoted company, is perhaps the largest such organization and warrants closer consideration.

CASE STUDY

The John Lewis Partnership is a £5 billion business with over 60,000 partners working in 26 department stores and 163 food shops. The first store was opened in London's Oxford Street in 1864 by the eponymous owner. The trust establishing the partnership was created by John Lewis's elder son Spedan Lewis once he had assumed control of the stores upon his father's death. Spedan Lewis had already shown himself to be an innovator internally, with the establishment of a committee specifically concerned with communications for staff. Externally he had positioned the organization strongly to the benefit of customers under the principle of 'never knowingly undersold'.

Since the establishment of the partnership in 1929 the profits have always been available for distribution amongst the partners. The ultimate purpose of the partnership is stated in its constitution as being the happiness of all its members, through their worthwhile and satisfying employment in a successful business. Since the partnership is owned in trust for its members, they share the responsibilities of ownership as well as its rewards: profit, knowledge and power. The monetary rewards of ownership are paid in the form of profit sharing, and in 2005 this amounted to 14 per cent of partners' pay. The total amount distributed was an impressive £106 million, with a further £80 million being set aside for the non-contributory pension scheme, while £70 million was retained for reinvestment in the business.

As founder of the partnership, through divesting himself of ownership, Spedan Lewis wanted to instil in partners an understanding that any benefits for them would depend entirely on the quality of service they delivered to the customers and the returns they were thus able to generate. He was very conscious that previous worker-cooperatives had tended to fail through losing sight of such commercial imperatives. To this day the partnership has continued to demonstrate impressive growth combined with an excellent reputation for service which is underpinned by the principle of being 'never knowingly undersold'. This principle is realized through dedicated teams in each shop charged with, and rewarded for, identifying lower prices in the local area.

The constitution provides partners with an involvement in the management of the organization through the mechanisms of a partnership board and the partnership council, which holds the chairman to account. As part of the commitment to open communication, partners are guaranteed anonymity when writing to the group's national or local magazines. This ensures that they can draw matters to the attention of the chairman and the other members of the management team, who in turn are required to respond to any letters addressed to them with complete honesty.

Source: John Lewis (2005).

WORKS COUNCILS

Not too far removed from a workers' cooperative, one way in which employees participate in the governance of their employer is through a works council. This can be defined as an institutionalized body for representative communication between an employer and employees in a single workplace.

There has been a long history of works councils, particularly in Europe, where they were given greater prominence with the passing of the European Works Council (EWC) Directive. In the UK this directive was implemented in early 2000 through the Transnational Information and Consultation of Employee Regulations 1999. This legislation complements the EWC Directive by effectively catering for works councils that operate at a national level.

The EWC Directive applies to all companies located in more than one EU Member State and with at least 1,000 employees in total. There is however no obligation for companies to establish an EWC unless either company management takes the initiative to do so, or employees (or their representatives) make a request. If it is deemed that a council is required, a negotiating body called the 'special negotiating body' (SNB) must first be established. The SNB consists of representatives of all the employees in the Member States in which the undertaking has operations, and it is the SNB's responsibility to negotiate an agreement for an EWC with the management of the company.

As with the Information and Consultation Directive that followed, there are provisions for much of the detail, including the composition of the EWC in terms of the number of members and so on; the functions and procedure for information and consultation; the venue, frequency and duration of EWC meetings; the financial and material resources to be allocated to the EWC; and the duration of the agreement and the procedure.

The expected subject matter in any discussions relates to those issues that apply across the national boundaries in which the company operates. An Annex to the Directive lists those topics on which the EWC has the right to be informed and consulted (for example the economic and financial situation of the business, its likely development, probable employment trends, the introduction of new working methods, and substantial organizational changes).

In practice few if any EWCs have been set up in the UK under the statutory model. However it is understood that the provisions of many agreements follow the statutory model quite closely. According to 'The UK experience of European Works Councils', a section of a report produced by the Department for Trade and Industry (DTI, 2003), a synthesis of the themes from various studies showed that:

Some companies have found them to be of value, even if management did have some initial doubts about the resource implications at the time they were established. Particular benefits identified in the research include better cross-business co-ordination among management teams and a better thought out corporate strategy. Less positive aspects include the increased bureaucracy involved in setting up and running an EWC and sometimes unfulfilled employee expectations about what an EWC might achieve.

ENCOURAGING EMPLOYEES TO BECOME SHAREHOLDERS

The number of companies that are completely owned by their employees is fairly small, but for many the logic of encouraging employees to cement their involvement with the organization, sharing in the rewards of success, is compelling. It is also an aspiration that is supported by governments in many Western democracies. This section therefore considers ways in which this is encouraged among those organizations with share capital to distribute.

One of the consequences of generating interest in share ownership and hence the share price is the evidence of a company's share price becoming more visibly on display, for instance on intranets, corporate websites and in reception areas of company offices. Indirectly therefore it becomes a means by which employees are encouraged to take an interest in how outsiders view the organization, and it should result in them looking at the broader picture rather than being solely internally focused.

That said, such an interest in and awareness of the external communication flows (both from and concerning the organization) makes it imperative that the messages going out are consistent with those sent to the employees directly. Moreover, it is not enough to communicate consistently: behaviour has to be consistent with the messages as well. One example of where this has to be handled very carefully is cost cutting. While messages about the control of costs will typically be well received by the investing publics, it will inevitably raise concerns among employees about job security. So it is important to resist the temptation to stress the benefits to one audience which will disappoint another, in those situations where there is little overlap between the two.

In the same way that the previous chapter demonstrated that the efforts of employees need to be directed towards satisfying customers and not just making employees happy, so it is with shareholders. Any scheme that seeks to motivate employees through the use of share capital clearly needs to set objectives that are consistent with the broader plans for the business, and be compatible with the ethos and culture of it.

Another important aspect is that encouraging employees to become shareholders introduces the need for a continuous programme of communications. Not all employees will be familiar with the ways of the stock market and so they may not always understand why the share price can fall as well as rise. Without some reassuring commentary or explanation as events unfold, many employees could be left uncertain about the benefits of shareholding, and in the worst case it could result in the scheme having the opposite effect of the motivation intended.

Share plans

In the UK there have been various initiatives over the years to support the aim of wider share ownership amongst employees. At any one time there are likely to be different schemes in operation with varying criteria. Some must be open to all employees and offer them tax breaks (potentially free of income and capital gains tax as well as national insurance contributions) if they take advantage of the scheme. The awarding of free shares may be linked to company, team or individual performance, and where the shares are held in trust for the employee the plans can assist with staff retention, as early leavers are likely to have to forfeit any shares given to them as employees.

Alternatively employees may be able to purchase shares in the company they work for through the granting of rights (known as share options) to buy a certain number of shares at a fixed price at a particular time in the future. Such schemes may be open to all employees or there may be plans aimed at motivating a specific group.

Given the culture of owning stocks and shares in the United States, it is not surprising that there have long been schemes with tax breaks (or 'qualified' in US tax terminology) to encourage participation in the company's success. As with the UK these schemes include variations on the themes of granting options to employees and giving them the right to purchase company stock using their own resources.

In addition things can be taken a stage further as some schemes involve retirement plans that allow the company to fund purchases of company stock on behalf of the employee. This connection with retirement plans was deemed to be extremely important by a study from Rutgers University (Kruse and Blasi, 2000). Douglas Kruse and Joseph Blasi found not only that companies with such plans increase sales, employment, and sales/employee by about 2.3 to 2.4 per cent per year over what would have been expected from those without them, but in addition they were more likely to be still in business several years later.

CASE STUDIES

Australia also has a number of alternative schemes, and a good example of their effectiveness comes from the Workplace website created by the Australian government. Two case studies are highlighted. The first deals with CEA, an electronics design company with approaching 300 employees operating out of Canberra, Adelaide, Melbourne and San Diego.

Having first introduced a share ownership plan back in 1998, CEA subsequently introduced an employee share option scheme whereby the number of options that were offered to employees was dependent on length of service, seniority, contribution to company performance and the position held in the company. One of the challenges faced by CEA was the complexity associated with the tax system, which required professional advice on the best way to set up their plan.

In addition, CEA faced the task of communicating the opportunities to employees. There will always be a certain number of staff who do not wish to be involved in an employee share ownership plan, even though it contains minimal risk for them. One reason is the perception of the plans as being complicated. Resolving these issues required the provision of as much information to employees about the plan as possible, as well as access to independent financial advisers. In the event the plan was taken up by 82 per cent of employees.

The company clearly believes that their employee share ownership plans have had, and continue to have, a significant and positive impact on the business throughout a period of strong growth. The evidence for this is one of the highest employee retention rates in Australian business and an excellent productivity record, even when compared to the highly competitive industry in which CEA operates. CEA uses employee share ownership to provide an atmosphere within the company where employees feel valued and are interested in the performance of the organization.

As far as the employees are concerned, they benefit from an increase in the satisfaction they receive from their job as well as an improvement in their personal financial situation. They like the idea of being able to invest in a company where they are able to influence the returns they receive. One of the most interesting observations of an employee was this:

> When the company first began I really felt like I was contributing to something greater than myself. Then, as the company grew and

my personal influence seemed to lessen, I found the employee share ownership plan supported my feeling of involvement and the worth of my work to the company as a whole.

The same employee also mentioned that employee share ownership at CEA contributed to a family atmosphere where employees felt supported and valued.

The second case study concerns the Australian division of a much larger company, the Compass Group. The intention of introducing a share ownership plan was similar to many other companies: to motivate staff and encourage them to have an interest in their company, while enabling them to share in the company's success. In the process Compass sought to attract as well as retain high-performing people.

Recognizing the importance of communication, Compass used an array of approaches supported by a dedicated communications team. The launch of the scheme involved a cascade process overseen by the HR function, which included an information leaflet distributed to all employees to explain the initiative and how to become a part of it. Subsequently, and on a regular basis, staff received 'Katch-up' newsletter (a quarterly magazine) and 'Stop Press' bulletin (a fortnightly newsletter) as well as access to updates and information on the company intranet.

The accent on communication enabled Compass to deal with the lack of familiarity and understanding amongst employees of employee share ownership plans (what they mean, how they work and the benefit for the employee), as well as the potentially demotivating effects arising from a falling share price.

OTHER STAKEHOLDERS

It is inevitable that discussion of employees and shareholders should lead on to the wider circle of stakeholders in an organization. Although less likely to be as directly affected by the successes and failures of the organization, these audiences can still influence its activities as well as being influenced by them. In many respects, this is a development of the discussion of corporate social responsibility in the previous chapter. It is therefore appropriate to consider what interests these audiences represent. These will inevitably vary in importance considerably between organizations, but the most common ones are considered below.

For many organizations the most influential stakeholder, setting aside employees, customers and shareholders, is the government, both national or local. Not only can it legislate in such a way as to curb or enhance various activities that the organization wishes to undertake, but it is also a notable beneficiary through taxation. Engaging in dialogue with government is consequently an important task to minimize adverse effects on the scope of an organization's activities. More positively, organizations can also work with and support government in the development of legislation that will assist other groups such as consumers.

Included under a broad heading of government are the various regulatory bodies that implement legislation, set standards and oversee the activities of organizations in particular sectors. In addition, there are many NGOs (non-governmental organizations) that operate at a national or international level, which while not being affiliated to governments can nevertheless lead thinking and developments in particular areas such human rights or the environment.

One of the ways in which debates about such topics unfold is through the media: the press, radio or television. Hence it is also important to ensure that good links are maintained with journalists and the various media owners. Those organizations that have a fully staffed press office will also tend to have people responsible for government liaison. In this way the organization hopes to keep abreast of developments as well as ensure that its voice is heard. The functions that carry out these duties are therefore similar to an investor relations department in that they are specialized in what they do, and there is no involvement for the vast majority of employees.

In contrast all employees are interacting with the general public everyday (not necessarily within the confines of their work) and can be said to be ambassadors for their employers in any activities not directly related to their employment. Over and above such interactions organizations have plenty of opportunities to demonstrate their sense of social responsibility through involvements nationally and locally. These include working formally with stakeholders such as charitable organizations, educational establishments, whole communities or groups concerned with a specific issue that the organization wishes to support.

The delivery of the organization's involvement in such matters may only require limited contribution from employees, for instance when the support is purely financial. However, in many instances it will require the direct efforts of those employees willing, say, to supervise an in-school bank, assist with the provision of facilities for disadvantaged children or raise funds for a charity. Involvements at a local level, whereby employees who work in a particular location support activities in that local community, can be a very powerful demonstration of an organization's commitment to CSR, especially given the extent to which customers and potential customers base their perceptions of that organization on the local presence. By participating in such activities employees can be said to be demonstrating engagement with the strategy of the organization and commitment to it.

A very good example of a marriage between a national effort and linkages to local communities has been the Tesco 'Computers for Schools' scheme. Organized and promoted nationally, the beneficiaries are the local schools that have been able to obtain free computers and related equipment, such as digital cameras, as a result of the collection of vouchers by those who shop in Tesco stores. The scheme has been in operation now for 14 years.

Education is clearly an important topic at national level, while primary and secondary schools are part of the fabric of local communities. This sector can also be considered as a stakeholder in business life at the tertiary level, notably through universities. Here, what is sometimes referred to as 'academia' can be considered to be a stakeholder as it is capable of influencing what organizations do and how they behave through the development of ideas, research and analysis. Another reason for organizations to become involved with academia and partner institutions is that they also represent a source of future employees.

Closer to the day-to-day activities of the organization are trade partners and suppliers. Apart from very specific transactional dealings between client and supplier, there is usually a mutual benefit in developing a longer-term relationship which is akin to the retention and development of employees.

Overall the sort of benefits that accrue from interacting with these other stakeholders include collaborative learning, identifying solutions to problems, avoiding conflict and developing a consensus for the future. One particularly good example comes from the West Midlands region in the UK, which is home to one of the larger building societies, the West Bromwich.

CASE STUDY

With 50 branches the West Bromwich Building Society operates in some of the country's most diverse communities. By adopting a genuine diversity programme it has been able to work with the local communities to develop new products and services (such as a mortgage that is compliant with sharia law for Muslims) well in advance of its competitors. The Society has also been able to attract the best staff from the different communities. Along with the efforts designed to extend the cultural awareness of staff at all levels, this recruitment has ensured that the Society is able to demonstrate on a practical level that it understands and meets the needs of existing and potential customers.

In turn, employees are then encouraged to support other organizations such as charities, local authorities, other regional building societies and companies in launching their own diversity programmes. The Society also uses broadcast media aimed at Asian consumers using their mother tongue, through advertising and tailored advice programmes.

The business case for working in the area of racial equality is defined in the corporate plan, and the financial benefits can be seen in the growth in customer numbers and the extent of the income generated from customers of ethnic origin, which is a source of revenue that still has tremendous potential for further growth.

INTELLECTUAL CAPITAL

Turning now to the notion of people and knowledge as capital, the discussion concerning intellectual capital (IC) embodies a desire to manage the sum total of the knowledge and information held within an organization. Gordon Petrash, partner at PricewaterhouseCoopers in Chicago and former global director of Intellectual Capital and Intellectual Asset Management at Dow Chemical Co, summarizes the situation as follows:

> Managing Intellectual Capital is when you take the three basic components of IC – human, organizational and customer/supplier – and make decisions with all three variables in the equation, rather than in a lineal progression … everything is considered in a multifunctional, multiperspective approach.
>
> (quoted in Madigan, 1999)

IC is therefore closely linked with the topic of knowledge management, which is discussed later in the book. As with knowledge management, the breadth of definitions of what constitutes IC is somewhat variable. What is common however is the desire to bring greater accuracy to the valuation of what might otherwise be treated in a set of accounts as intangibles or goodwill.

Steven Wallman, senior non-resident fellow at the Brookings Institution and former commissioner, US Securities & Exchange Commission, is quoted (also in Madigan) as saying in 1999:

> You can't manage what you can't measure. We are missing, in a major way, some of the real drivers of both wealth and cost in companies by excluding a whole range of things that are normally subsumed under the label of Intellectual Capital.

And to quote from Reichheld (1996):

> Today's accounting systems often mask the fact, but inventories of experienced customers, employees, and investors are a company's most valuable assets. Their combined knowledge and experience comprise a firm's entire Intellectual Capital. Yet these invaluable assets are vanishing from corporate balance sheets at an alarming rate, decimating growth and earnings potential as they go. In a typical (Western) company today, customers are defecting at the rate of 10 to 30 percent per year; employee turnover rates of 15 to 25% are common; and average investor churn now exceeds 50 percent per year. How can any company be expected to grow a profitable business when 20 to 50% of the company's most valuable inventory vanishes without trace each year?

In order to realize the ambition of a more precise valuation of such assets, it is necessary to consider what might be included as IC. For some IC is about the value of items such as trademarks, patents, licences and brand names. It is therefore an alternative to the description of intellectual property, and is an area where historically there have been more attempts to incorporate valuations in balance sheets. Sometimes these elements are categorized together as structural capital, and described in terms of the items that do not leave the buildings when the employees go home. It can therefore also include such things as processes, databases and information systems.

Others will include in their definition of IC something called customer capital, which is made up of the value of the customer relationships that the organization enjoys through loyalty to that organization and its products and services. Efforts in this regard have been given a boost as more organizations seek to put a value on the brands available to them. Such valuations could clearly be extended to other audiences, such as suppliers, where the continuing relationship is extremely important to the continuing activities of organization, especially one involved in manufacturing.

More generally IC is deemed to include some aspects of what is known by the people in the organization as well. So this is the value that walks out of the door with employees, and in service organizations can clearly constitute the vast bulk of any definition of IC.

Although he does not use precisely the same definitions, Sveiby in 'The invisible balance sheet' used the terms 'internal structure' and 'external structure' to encompass those items that others would describe as structural capital and customer capital. The third 'family' he labelled as individual competence: the ability of people to act in various situations. It therefore includes skills, education, experience, values and social skills that are deployed in developing the internal and external structures.

While competence cannot be owned by the organization, perhaps the strongest argument for trying to include a valuation in the balance sheet is the simple difficulty of envisaging that organization without any people. Sveiby goes on to argue that part of the cost of this arrangement is in the commitment (not shown in a balance sheet) to pay pensions, golden parachutes, redundancy payments and other monies upon departure from the organization by way of acknowledgement of the contribution made.

Another way of looking at the knowledge possessed by an organization is to split it in the way sometimes used in knowledge management into tacit and explicit. Although there is an argument that information only becomes knowledge in people's heads, many use the word tacit to describe this form of knowledge and describe everything else as being explicit. Tacit knowledge is therefore the product of people's skills, experience and values, whereas explicit knowledge is that which is recorded on paper, in databases and so on.

Knowledge management is particularly concerned with the flows between tacit and explicit knowledge as they represent an attempt to capture and possibly codify information, skills and experience for others to use. It is therefore less concerned with the tacit-to-tacit transfer, which is about sharing knowledge between people, although clearly this is an aspect that is critical in other areas such a team building.

HUMAN CAPITAL

Given that this book is concerned primarily with employees, the extent to which they may be considered to make up some of the capital of an organization warrants a more detailed discussion. The Chartered Institute of Personnel and Development (CIPD) defines human capital as the contribution of people (their skills and knowledge) in the production of goods and services.

As was noted earlier there are now expectations that companies in the UK will include a commentary on human capital in their operating and financial reviews, although there has not been any prescription for what should be covered in such a commentary. Inevitably, it is a subject that creates a lot of debate about what should be included and how things should be measured.

Some of the important aspects relating to employees are best dealt with in a qualitative sense, which immediately makes them difficult to measure. Examples of the more qualitative judgements made about people range from an assessment of their current competencies, through an indication of commitment to the values of the organization, and on to their potential contribution to the organization going forward.

One person who has attempted to overcome such difficulties is Mayo, who in 2001 outlined a detailed framework linking the qualitative assessment of competencies to financial valuation. In his concept of 'human asset worth', the value of an individual's human capital is defined as equal to 'Employment Cost × Individual Asset Multiplier/1,000', where the Individual Asset Multiplier is defined as a weighted average assessment of some of the relevant factors. The important thing is that it represented an attempt to focus on the value creation of employees. However, given the context-specific nature of such assessments, there is a limit to the extent to which such measures can be compared across organizations.

The understandable desire to benchmark such measures does raise the question more generally about the efficacy of having measures that apply to all organizations. While it is one thing to illuminate a report by recording the contribution made by people, it is another to be able to do so consistently across a diverse array of organizations. There is merit in being able to strive for consistency across organizations in the same sector or of the same type, but even here there are still challenges that need to be overcome.

One of the first challenges or debates to be settled is the basis of valuation, given that there are a number of alternatives. Some people would propose a valuation that is cost-based: that is, the historic cost of acquiring people and skills spread over the expected length of service. It could therefore include recruitment and training costs. However, the question remains whether this is a good guide to the present capabilities of the organization.

Possibly more helpful is the notion of market value, although this is of course only more helpful in those sectors where there is a ready market for people and skills. Equally, it cannot always be said that the cost of attracting individuals always equates to the value of their role to the organization. This issue is indicative of a broader dilemma whereby the data that can be more readily collated and are financially based not only have wider applicability but also have more credibility in the eyes of the accounting fraternity. Yet, almost by definition, staying with what can already be easily done means that the frontiers of genuinely measuring the contribution of people will not be rolled back that far.

The alternative approach of considering the income potential of individuals has the advantage of relating more closely to the worth of the organization, although it is a task that is inevitably made easier for those functions and roles, such as sales, that are more immediately linked to income. This then also brings us back to the merits and shortcomings of qualitative assessments addressed above.

In the debates that pit flexibility of use against comparability and organizationally specific against generic, it is at least helpful to have a framework of the sorts of measures that potentially could be used. Such a framework was provided in a report by Neely *et al* (2002) of the Centre for Business Performance at Cranfield School of Management in 2002 for the Council for Excellence in Management and Leadership (CEML). This offered measures of management and leadership under five different headings.

First there is morale. This covers the reporting of accidents, sickness and absences across all levels in an organization. In addition it was suggested that turnover be recorded for directors and managers separately from all employees. Also included under this heading is a measure of employee satisfaction, as derived from a staff opinion survey.

The next heading is motivation. Under this come the completion rates for appraisals, the percentage of jobs with job descriptions, written statements of objectives and documented appraisals that have been agreed. Staff opinion surveys would then contribute by way of the understanding employees have of the organization's vision and strategy. As with turnover above, working hours and retention rates would be recorded separately for directors and managers and for employees as a whole.

The third grouping is investment in people and this is represented by training as well as benchmarked remuneration levels, director/manager remuneration as a percentage of the total bill for remuneration, and the HR spend per employee.

Long-term development represents the fourth heading. This includes an assessment of the current and potential management and leadership capability, an indication of the management and leadership skills gap; the percentage of jobs with emergency cover and with long-term cover; the percentage of job holders with agreed development plans; the proportion of jobs with competencies that have been audited; and training days held.

The final area is external perception, which is represented by such factors as the ratio of job applications to vacancies and of job offers to acceptances.

As is inevitably the case, some of the more useful items are those that are more difficult to value, the main point being that increasingly efforts are being made to attach a value where previously no attempts have been made. As Sveiby also pointed out, care needs to be exercised in relating the valuation of the assets in the balance sheet to the market value of a company. Using Nokia as an example, he demonstrated the fluctuating market value of an organization when it is extremely unlikely that there was a comparable fluctuation in the value of the human capital.

The measures of management and leadership above also serve to underscore the importance of drawing upon a range of sources, and the benefits that can accrue from the appropriate functions (finance, HR, market research and so on) working together to produce the most relevant and meaningful measures.

CONCLUSIONS

The interaction between owners, managers and employees can be as relevant to the continued success of an organization as the interaction with customers. To facilitate the coordination of direction and effort there are benefits in giving employees the opportunity to participate directly in the rewards available when the organization is successful. There are a number of ways in which this can be achieved when the organization is a company with share capital.

Yet irrespective of the nature of ownership it is still possible to confer upon employees varying levels of participation in the management of the organization. In addition it is also clear that there have to be effective channels of communication to ensure that the efforts of employees are directed wisely, and that they are able to participate in the management of the organization as befits their capacity as owners.

At the same time, the recognition of the importance of employees to all organizations has led to efforts to measure their contribution. In accounting and economic terms this has led to the blurring of the distinction between labour and capital. In order to provide effective measures for financial reporting the debate continues about the most relevant ways of collation and recording data. In practice it is always likely to be a combination of various sources and types, drawn from financial accounts, HR records, research surveys and other sources.

4 Employee research and the communications context

INTRODUCTION

Up to this point there have been various references in the book to communication. Employee research assists with the development of communication; it is itself a means of communication while it is also an activity that needs to be supported by other communications channels. It is therefore highly relevant to consider the main ways in which communication occurs in an organization. Communication is after all the means by which the demands of the organization and the potential contribution of the employee can be aligned or calibrated. It facilitates the adjustment of priorities as well as the development of individuals and the functioning of teams to maximum advantage.

Given that the context is one of communication both to and from those who manage the organization and those who work in it, a broad categorization of activities separates those channelled through representatives from those that can take place directly. This chapter develops this categorization and considers the principal ways in which communication takes place. In so doing it also considers the opportunities for these channels to complement and be supported by the use of research techniques. Additionally, since an organization will communicate with other, external audiences in ways that could influence employees indirectly there is coverage of the main 'indirect' communications channels.

REPRESENTATIVES

Turning first to communication via representatives, it is possible to subdivide these into those who are independent of the organization's management and those who are part of the organization's management team.

Independent representatives

Typically in an organization where the workforce has representatives they will meet with the management team to discuss issues in a structured environment such as a committee, joint working party, council or forum. Although such bodies can deal with issues beyond those prescribed in collective bargaining agreements, the extent to which this is possible is dependent on the mutual trust that develops between the parties involved, a process that can of course take time and effort both at and away from the committee meeting room.

The benefit to employees of voicing their concerns through a representative in this way is that it gives them licence to air views that they may not feel able to assert more directly, for fear of retribution. This in turn gives envoys the challenge of ensuring that the views they present are indeed representative of the workforce as a whole and not just of those prepared to speak up, or those with the loudest voices.

The most obvious examples of representatives acting on behalf of the workforce in these situations are trade unions and staff associations which represent those employees who are their members, both collectively and individually (for example, representing them at tribunals). The members of these bodies are likely to feature prominently as information and consultation representatives under the new regulations (discussed later in the book) which will have the effect of widening the pool of employees who act in such a capacity.

Where trade unions are recognized by an organization for the purposes of collective bargaining, they clearly play an integral part in the life of that organization. Indeed, even when an activity such as a company-wide employee survey is planned and implemented by external parties such as market research agencies it is important that the relevant union is consulted in advance to maximize the participation of the workforce.

Management representatives

The role of line managers and supervisory staff employed directly by an organization is particularly pertinent to the discussion about the way in which information is disseminated. Although by definition these are part of the organization's management structure, they can also be said to act as representatives of the employees they oversee. If the system is functioning well they should act as the fulcrum in the communication balance between individual employees and those in management who are responsible for the direction of the organization.

Although there is much discussion of the benefits of flat organizational structures, with minimal management hierarchy, it seems safe to assume that organizations of size and substance will continue to operate these chains of command. Apart from anything else they offer a means of identifying future management potential. The 'assault course' that is corporate life does mean that (without recourse to recruitment externally) potential leaders can be given incremental responsibilities and an assessment can be made of those who will best handle responsibility for the entire organization.

In addition, flat structures, while attractive in some respects (being the antithesis of a long chain of command with the attendant danger that those at the top are too far removed from the 'coal face'), do not afford the perception of progress and potential career development that is more readily satisfied by a series of promotions.

Given the probability that many organizations will continue to operate a hierarchical structure, there will remain a need for management at each level to communicate with those for whom they are responsible. The challenge, according to Jocelyn Johnson (2000) is for managers to demonstrate greater empathy with their subordinates. She reported on a large-scale study amongst managers and their colleagues in the public sector. This showed that the managers were considerably more positive about the work climate and culture than those who worked for them. It is consequently difficult to expect managerial and supervisory staff to accurately report back the views of those they are responsible for because they may lack empathy for how they actually feel about such matters. Hence it is important to have available the means of acquiring feedback independently from the management structure as well as through it.

Examples of ways in which there is a flow of information between employees and the organization and which depend on the line manager are examined in the following sections.

Briefing meetings

Frequently used to disseminate information on major developments or updates on progress and performance, these meetings are an opportunity for teams to gather in person and discuss local issues and problems. In some organizations such meetings are a regular feature, and there is a mix of local and strategic topics. When the topics are about the organization as a whole they may also involve the use of some of the direct communication methods (such as videos) discussed later in this chapter. In essence these meetings are about face-to-face communication, understanding, informing staff of developments and decisions that might affect them and gaining feedback.

Among the qualities required of the manager who leads the meetings is commitment to ensure that such meetings take place according to a timetable that accommodates as many of those who need to be involved as possible. This in turn assumes an ability to plan and sequence the meetings, which can be assisted by the creation of a routine so that everyone knows the days and times that they can expect such meetings to take place. Where a routine has been established, there will be occasions when the manager is unable to attend, in which case the commitment and planning has to extend to organizing an appropriate deputy to lead the meeting.

The presentational capabilities of the manager are of course crucial to the effectiveness of getting the key messages across in a way that is relevant to the group of employees. When such meetings are part of a cascade process this is particularly important, otherwise the message received by those at the end of the sequence will be far removed from how it started out. (With apologies to those unfamiliar with pre-decimal currency, one of the best examples of how this can go wrong is an apocryphal tale from military circles. A general wished to relay the message, 'Send reinforcements; we are going to advance.' Unfortunately, there was bemused reaction when the final recipients in the chain were informed, 'Send three and four-pence, we are going to a dance.')

In addition, the manager also determines how effective such a forum is for discussion and communication up the line to the management team. Apart from the communication skills of the manager, there must be a willingness to put aside personal concerns about how the message, which will sometimes not be palatable to senior management, reflects on the bearer. There is also an obligation on the part of the manager to ensure that actions are taken arising from any feedback gathered. Where responsibility for a particular area or subject lies outside the team giving the feedback, this requires at a minimum that the manager of that team ensures the feedback reaches the relevant recipients.

The meetings can of course be used to advantage as a means of communicating across the organization. For instance, the manager of one team might describe their duties and responsibilities to another team with a view to promoting closer cooperation between the two functions. Here the ambassadorial qualities of the manager need to be in evidence.

Appraisals

Although not normally regarded as a medium of communication between the organization and employees, the formal review meetings that are an essential component of any appraisal system do of course mean that employees learn the extent to which they are valued. Ideally this information is communicated informally in the normal course of business, although the review meetings, which should be at least an annual event and preferably take place two or three times a year, create the opportunity for progress to be recorded against specific objectives as well as in personal development.

As well as giving individual feedback, such discussions are important in placing the performance of individuals in the context of the wider group of which they are a part. As a consequence individuals should learn how well the group as a whole is performing, and may well receive an indication how their own performance compares with others in the group.

Feedback for the purpose of appraisals is of course not limited to line managers. Appraisals are an opportunity for managers to collate the views of their peers as well as those of the person being appraised. Somewhat less common is the practice of including the views of an individual's subordinates. This approach of obtaining the views of the complete spectrum of those who come into contact with the individual is generally known as 360-degree feedback, and requires high levels of integrity to ensure that it retains credibility.

However the appraisal process is practised, the attendant formal review is likely to take the form of a face-to-face meeting, with the consequent opportunity for the employee to voice observations and concerns of a wider nature. The extent to which this feedback is passed on or acted upon will depend on the line manager who receives this information – much in the same way as was noted above regarding briefing meetings.

DIRECT COMMUNICATIONS

Direct communications are those media that do not depend on intermediaries such as representatives or line managers, and provide a means by which the entire workforce can be addressed in the same way. It is important to consider these as supplementing, rather than competing with, other forms of communication. Much in the same way that an organization will address its external audiences through a combination of methods (such as television advertising, direct mail and PR), internal communications also benefit from using a variety of media which complement each other.

Conferences and other large-scale meetings

Occupying some of the central ground between other direct media and the briefing meetings for smaller units and teams referenced above, conferences and other large-scale meetings will typically be addressed by senior executives and used for more strategic messages. Gathering everyone possible from the organization at least ensures that the same messages are received by all concerned. Indeed, the use of video links means that employees at different locations can be party to the same event.

Unlike other direct media discussed below, these meetings offer the opportunity in theory to incorporate some element of feedback and consultation. Indeed they are sometimes referred to as town hall meetings precisely because of the intention to gather the views and opinions of those attending. One particular example of this practice by Sears is referred to in Chapter 2 when discussing the employee–customer profit chain. The innovation employed by Sears was to combine this style of meeting with the use of learning maps. The latter provided the content and required people to make use of their analytical skills, whereas the format of the meetings facilitated the conversion of that learning into action.

Whatever the format of such meetings, they demand considerable efforts in planning and execution given the sheer number of participants, the time devoted to them and the fact that employees will typically have had little time to digest the information received before being asked to respond. It can therefore make sense to have a separate channel (distinct from as well as subsequent to the meeting itself) in order to collate feedback on, say, the content, handling and effectiveness of the session.

Video and other broadcast media

The use of video has long offered a complementary as well as an alternative medium for communicating corporate information and strategies. It is complementary in the sense that, for instance, video footage can be deployed to great effect at conferences or team meetings. In addition, it is a cost-effective way of encapsulating the content and atmosphere of conferences for the benefit of those unable to attend in person. Yet it can also be a stand-alone medium, suited to communicating information and guidance on topics that warrant reinforcement with repeated viewing, such as health and safety issues.

The economics of producing video tapes (and more recently DVDs) depend on the number of copies required, with the marginal costs of each extra one minimal in comparison with the cost of producing the original. Given the costs involved with video production, and the potential impact on the viewing audience, it makes eminent sense to undertake some research to check out the strategy and execution before distribution, much in the same way as research is an integral part of advertising development.

Assuming that there is an effective method of distribution, one of the major benefits that can be realized from video is the opportunity for everyone in the organization to view the content at the same time. What has encouraged some organizations to go beyond video and to set up their own broadcast media or television channel using satellite technology is the requirement to do this while also communicating in a timely fashion. So where there is a premium on speed and timeliness of information, to ensure that people in the organization are able to keep pace with developments, investments in the technology can be justified.

The use of video and television does imply that communication is one-way: from management to the workforce, although if a showing is incorporated into a team meeting it is possible that there can be some discussion and feedback via the person leading the meeting. One of the limiting factors in such arrangements is the size of any group that has access to a television monitor and video or DVD player.

Meanwhile the profusion of desktop PCs along with the development of intranets (internet protocol or IP networks) has resulted in many other possibilities opening up. Apart from it being a store of knowledge and information, an intranet is also a potential delivery channel for video content. This means that live events can be broadcast to every desktop, and it also opens up possibilities for conferencing between people in disparate locations. Inevitably those organizations operating at the forefront of the technology such as Cisco are leading the way in using it for the purposes of internal communications. There is a clear cost advantage of using these channels over their predecessors, and there is even more scope for saving time and money when they are contrasted with gathering people together in conferences and meetings.

However, it has to be remembered that there are still many organizations, indeed many jobs in a variety of organizations, where the desktop PC, let alone the laptop or notebook, is not commonplace. In addition, by relying on a channel that delivers content to individuals, the need for group interaction, discussion and feedback can be overlooked to the potential detriment of the team and possibly the organization as a whole.

Intranets

Increasingly, written material that once would have been printed and distributed is now to be found electronically. It may still be distributed to individuals, say in the form of a CD, but it is as likely to be found on shared network drives and intranets. A clear benefit of being able to access information on an intranet is that it can be updated frequently without incurring the printing and distribution costs of hard copy versions. This also gives the organization considerable flexibility in the content that it makes available to employees, and provides for more open access to information across the organization.

Other benefits include the financial gains from cost savings in dealing with technical support queries electronically via FAQs (documents detailing frequently asked questions with answers) and a reduction in expenditure in terms of implementation, training and running costs. In addition, the technology involved means an intranet can sit alongside legacy systems without requiring large amounts of capital expenditure.

The in-house equivalent of the internet has been around since the mid-1990s, and through making information available across organizations has the potential to be a force for democracy and decentralization. With some of the gains inevitably comes some cost; functions with the responsibility for centralized libraries will either have been the champions of an intranet or seen their jobs disappear as a consequence.

The obvious content for an intranet consists of such items as directories, thereby avoiding the problems of always having something that is out of date as soon as it is published. More debatably, an intranet should offer some external sources of information. Access to the internet and the worldwide web is contentious in some organizations. While it opens up the possibilities for accessing information and ideas, there is nevertheless some reluctance because of expectations of abuse and time-wasting. The corporate view that is taken on such matters is in itself an interesting comment on the issue of trust within the organization.

Essentially, most employees will respond positively to being entrusted with something, and will be reasonable in their usage, much in the same way that they have been with the telephone. What is required is guidance on what is acceptable, and many organizations have dealt with this situation by requiring employees to sign up to a code setting out the responsibilities attached to being given such access.

In considering the content available on an intranet site, the challenge is to identify what has sufficient relevance to the maximum number of people. Indeed, there can be the danger with something like an intranet that it is assumed to be the answer to all problems, with the consequence that it becomes overburdened with information that is not of interest. Without adequate controls the information may also be presented in such a way that it is no more accessible than what went before it. In addition, it is quite possible for an intranet to be developed quite separately from, and hence not fit with, the other communications media used by the organization.

It is therefore critical that an intranet should be established with the same planning and testing rigours that would be applied to any other new system, along with the opportunity for users to comment on developments. This can be done in advance of implementation through such techniques as usability testing, or subsequently, through other feedback channels.

When deployed successfully, an intranet can become a strategic tool that facilitates the sharing of best practice and provides the opportunity to improve service to customers. This is particularly true where the intranet assists the organization to span functional as well as international boundaries.

As with all such developments it is important not simply to expect it to just do the same things in a different way: for example, by transferring the existing paper library into an electronic form. The opportunity is there to do new things as well, not least of which is assisting the collaboration between fellow employees. As such the technology is the facilitator not the arbiter, and the organizational and human factors should be at the forefront in guiding any developments. With more organizations thinking about the integration of data and voice traffic on networks it is not surprising to find that some supplement the information available from an intranet by providing the facility to listen to pre-recorded and regularly changed bulletins about matters of interest on an internal telephone system.

Whether the technological developments do represent genuine advances or not, they have been accompanied by additions to the vocabulary. So there are webinars, which are seminars (or lectures or workshops) transmitted over the web. Quite often used for training, the event can be stored as a file and accessed by anyone who wishes to at a later time. Unlike a webcast, which is closer to being a web equivalent of a television broadcast, a webinar has the advantage of being interactive.

Another development occasioned by the technology is a blog or web log. Compiled by the blogger (a person who blogs), this is a journal that is posted online and which has the possibility of adding interesting content to the site as well as prompting debate and discussion on any issues raised. Microsoft, for instance, specifically encourages the use of blogs particularly in the area of development projects so that a wider audience can be informed of progress.

E-mail

Rather than relying on employees to visit an intranet, organizations can send information direct to individuals via e-mail. Of course the message could simply be an invitation or direction to the intranet to view new content onscreen (much in the same way that a poster would invite employees to a meeting in the non-electronic equivalent).

For those organizations without intranets, e-mail will be an important medium of communication in its own right. In addition, it is of course a medium that facilitates two-way communication, so that recipients of any message can immediately engage in discussion if so invited. One point to be borne in mind here is the potential reluctance of people to make their comments directly, particularly in respect of more controversial issues, when this medium does not offer them the cloak of anonymity. Equally, care has to be exercised so that the other extreme, whereby the sender may potentially be overwhelmed with responses, is catered for through the use of a dedicated address to which replies can be sent.

As with intranets, there can be a danger that those who have the means to communicate in this way make the mistake of assuming that everyone in the organization has access to similar technology. So whether the scene is a production line, a retail shop or even a bank branch, people may at best have restricted access to a PC, requiring communication to be tailored to their circumstances.

Magazines and newsletters

Many organizations produce in-house magazines or newspapers/newsletters. These represent another way in which corporate messages can be communicated to all employees. However, it is important that the medium does not become associated completely with a management perspective, as this can dilute the willingness to read or accept the content.

Nokia is an example of a company that produces such a magazine called *Nokia People*. It is published in the four most common languages in Nokia, English, Finnish, Chinese and German, eight times a year, and has a worldwide circulation in excess of 50,000 copies. As well as providing coverage of business stories and achievements it also devotes space to people stories and such matters as community involvement.

By extending the scope of such publications to social and personal news, the editorial board does depend on readers contributing directly to the content of the publication. The extent to which readers take up this opportunity will depend, as it does with other forms of soliciting feedback (notably research surveys) on the perception as to what will happen as a result. Clearly, if the editor is reluctant to publish contributions that are critical of the organization or no one ever takes any notice of what is written, however often it gets mentioned, the supply of contributors will quickly dry up.

Posters and notice boards

While there has been a sizeable shift to their electronic equivalents, it is worth mentioning that there is still a role for the more traditional method of communicating via posters and notice boards. They will continue to be important both where employees do not have access to electronic media as well as a supplement to other means of communicating.

Clearly the location of a poster or notice board is crucial to its effectiveness in being seen by those for whom it is intended. It is also a medium that can suffer from lack of maintenance and overload.

Company booklets

One example of a company booklet is the type of literature handed out as part of the induction process to give new recruits useful information about working in the organization. Then there are handbooks for all employees detailing company rules, policies and procedures, benefits and contact details. In the printed form such documents tend to err on the side of containing information that does not need to be updated too frequently.

Suggestion schemes

Although common in organizations, suggestion schemes are different from all of the other direct channels described above in that the primary intent is not to inform employees but to solicit thoughts and ideas from individual employees. The manner in which suggestions are dealt with can of course have a motivating or demotivating effect on that individual, but it is one of the few channels designed specifically for communication from employee to organization, albeit with a limited frame of reference.

There are many ways in which organizations seek to encourage employees to contribute suggestions about how improvements might be made. The principal requirements of any scheme are that suggestions are dealt with promptly (a response time of a week should be achievable) and in a way that is seen to be fair and reward those who offer worthwhile suggestions. In so doing it has to be recognized that some individuals may prefer to remain anonymous.

Dealing with suggestions promptly in turn requires those entrusted with making a decision to be empowered by the organization and accepting of the responsibility placed upon them. This raises the question whether employees should be permitted to make suggestions about their immediate job or team that qualify for an award, or whether that is something that should be a part of their role anyway. In addition, where employees make suggestions as to how improvements can be made in other areas, there is always the concern that such ideas may be greeted by almost a xenophobic, 'not invented here' type of attitude, or dismissed as having been considered and discarded some time before.

As can be seen with other communication channels, a suggestion scheme benefits from being seen to be acted upon and suffers if it is not. If handled badly it may therefore create as many problems as it seeks to solve. As well as encouraging suggestions through a variety of channels (e-mail, voice mail, fax, post and so on), there should be publicity for all suggestions in order to acknowledge the contributions as well as to encourage others. Indeed, some ideas may not themselves be that useful but can spark a thought by somebody else who ends up with a successful innovation.

Grievance procedures

A formal system for handling grievances is another example of a channel designed to convey messages from the individual to the management of the organization. Again it operates within a very specific frame of reference, but on this occasion is a system that ideally is never used at all on the basis that other channels of communication through managerial and supervisory staff should have been able to resolve the concerns raised.

KNOWLEDGE MANAGEMENT

Ultimately the aggregation of all sources of information can be described in terms of knowledge management. Most people recognize that raw data needs to be translated into information, and that for any value to be derived from that information it has to be capable of being applied. Yet there are a variety of definitions of what constitutes knowledge management and the practice of it will probably be unique to each organization.

The philosophy behind such a development is inspired by the desire to create an environment in which the information is not only applied (that is, turned in to knowledge), but also fosters continuous learning. It therefore also encompasses the knowledge and learning of individual employees as well as the corporate sources.

The businesses that adopt such an approach therefore regard knowledge as a resource to be valued in its own right. As a consequence the development and sharing of knowledge is something that warrants its own space in corporate life. To quote Thomas A Stewart (1997), 'Because knowledge has become the single most important factor of production, managing intellectual assets has become the single most important task of business.'

THE COMMUNICATIONS MIX

In the main, methods of communicating directly with employees do not allow for a dialogue: they are principally the means by which an organization provides information and seeks to exhort employees to do more or different things. The way in which the message is received is critical to the way in which it is responded to. Therefore being aware of the issues that are uppermost in the minds of employees at any one time is something of a Holy Grail for communicators. An accurate understanding of these issues could for instance influence the timing of any communication, if it is identified that there might be a better time to send the message out. Alternatively, the message could anticipate concerns of employees and marry the message content with solutions to those concerns.

In many respects the challenges faced by those charged with responsibility for internal communications were answered by Orwell's creation in *1984* of the Thought Police: 'How often, or on what system, the Thought Police plugged in on any individual wire was guesswork. It was even conceivable that they watched everybody all the time. But at any rate they could plug in your wire whenever they wanted to.' While no one would go so far as to say that there should be a corporate version of the Thought Police as envisaged by Orwell, internal communications is not simply about determining the message to be put across to employees, it is also about judging the mood of the audience and anticipating how the messages will be received.

The impact of any communication is a function of the way in which it is delivered and perceived as much as it is a function of the content contained within it. It is therefore highly desirable to be able to tap in to the mood of the workforce in order to position any communication effectively.

CASE STUDY

A leading retail bank explored several avenues in an attempt to identify a solution to this need for proactive feedback. For instance, the in-house journal had a small network of correspondents charged with providing material that reflected the activities and perspectives of employees in different regions. The regional training centres were also seen to represent a useful 'melting pot' of staff from a wide area who would, over the duration of a two or three-day course, talk openly to tutors about life in the bank.

Neither of these avenues met the need, as there was reluctance to get involved on the part of those being asked to be intermediaries

---

in this 'trafficking' of information, either because it represented an additional workload or because it was felt that there was an element of 'telling tales'. The Catch 22 here was that if the individuals expressing the views were told what would happen to any comments they made they would clam up, while if they were not told and spoke freely, the correspondents and tutors felt guilty about saying too much.

Meanwhile, an internal telephone unit was set up and resourced with the help of external and independent researchers, largely with a view to conducting surveys amongst employees. While this was successful in terms of the volume of work that went through the unit, the costs of undertaking what would amount to a substantial, continuous study militated against using the unit for the purpose of tracking those 'top of mind' issues amongst employees.

The advent of a company-wide intranet opened up the possibility of using a chat room so that staff could initiate discussions on the topics that were concerning them, as benevolent a version of the Thought Police as might be imagined. Unfortunately the bank shortly afterwards received an approach which led to a takeover battle, and although there was a lengthy and spirited defence, it ultimately resulted in the bank being taken over. Inevitably during the defence, which involved a change in the senior management team, the intranet became so overwhelmed with related topics and observations that the chat room facility was closed down. However, it had demonstrated that within sensible parameters it represented a barometer of the depth and breadth of feelings that were uppermost in the minds of employees at any one time.

When considering the mix of communications media to be used in any situation, it is also important to recognize the way in which employees are being bombarded with messages from many directions, much as any other audience is in this day and age. Unfortunately, in some organizations there is a belief that because a message has been sent out that it has been received and will be acted upon by all recipients. The reality is that there is leakage or wastage from the point at which the communication has been sent. It can almost be guaranteed that not everybody will have received it: no one channel is perfect and awareness of 100 per cent is very rarely, if ever, achieved in any field.

Even when the message has been received there will inevitably be variations in the way in which it is interpreted and acted upon. Hence it is necessary to check the take-out from any communications exercise as well as to identify how well different channels have performed in delivering the content of the message.

INDIRECT COMMUNICATIONS

Indirect methods describe those where the employees are an audience for the communication but not necessarily the principal one. This section is not therefore concerned, as some might have anticipated, with corporate gossip or the rumour mill. Although frequently shown in surveys to be a valued source of information by employees (even if it is not a channel through which they want to receive information), rumour/gossip flourishes because the organization allows it to inhabit a vacuum by virtue of the ineffectiveness of more formal channels of communication.

The concern of this section is those communications which almost by definition, if employees are not the primary audience, are aimed at external audiences. Given the point above about rumour and gossip, it is clearly sensible to make available such communications to employees so that they are clear how the organization is presenting itself to other audiences. The simple act of doing this will also help to eliminate any dissonance that can arise if the organization appears to be saying one thing externally and another thing to its workforce.

Advertising

Above-the-line advertising, notably that on television, is a particular example whereby the organization is addressing the general public, and in the course of so doing will be communicating with its own employees. Indeed, some advertising campaigns specifically portray employees and even go as far as to make employees the 'heroes'. An example is the advertising by Direct Line, which ran a campaign in which call centre staff were shown literally as superheroes from television and film (for example, *Charlie's Angels*) who went to great lengths to assist customers with their problems.

Other organizations (Asda/Walmart and ABN Amro are recent examples) cast their own employees in advertisements. In the UK the most famous example of this is probably the Halifax. Seeking to take on the traditional retail banks, it decided to position itself and communicate as a retailer. The decision was taken that all advertising would focus on the value of its services, and that it would target customers from the clearing banks. It also wanted to use advertising that would help motivate a customer-facing workforce. Out of this came the 'Staff as Stars' campaign featuring real Halifax staff, and the success of the first advertisement starring Howard Brown launched a second career for him as the face of the Halifax.

Although typically it is organizations in the services sector such as banks, utility companies, supermarkets and airlines that use advertising in this way (reflecting the fact that the delivery of a service by employees is effectively what determines the success or otherwise of those organizations), it is surprising just how many advertisements in any one break do show the interaction between an employee and a customer.

When this is done well there is scope for impressing both customers and employees. Occasionally, advertising can attempt to appeal to customers by poking fun at or belittling employees (any advertising that pokes fun at or belittles customers is of course taking that organization into very dangerous territory). The clear danger here is that employees may not share the joke and will feel slighted, with an immediate impact on morale and pride in their work.

Even rarer is that classic example of advertising that succeeds in alienating all the primary audiences. The best example in recent times is the advertising by Sainsbury's in support of its 1998 'Value to shout about' campaign, featuring John Cleese. While people may not have been aware of the sequence of events that led up to those adverts appearing on screen (including the withdrawal of the principal character around whom the original strategy had been devised, and the replacement by Cleese) what is remembered is Cleese as a store manager hectoring the customers in a way that embarrassed the workforce.

Finally, it is worth mentioning that some organizations take the opportunities afforded by television advertising to go one stage further and address their employees directly. By using one of the cheaper ad breaks (for instance, early on a Sunday morning) it is possible to communicate to all employees irrespective of how widely spread they may be around the country. This is an approach that has been favoured by companies in the financial sector, such as banks and insurance companies where the workforce is spread over a national network of offices and branches.

The cost of the air time means that the message does not have to be restricted to the normal length of an advertisement, although clearly it still has to remain succinct. A common reason for adopting this approach is to showcase a new advertising campaign, so there can still be benefit derived from other audiences who may happen to be viewing at that time.

Annual reports and accounts

A requirement for publicly quoted companies, and good practice for many other organizations, the annual report is an opportunity to reflect on progress and to set out aspirations for the future. Although the primary audience for quoted companies will be the investing public, even where employees are not themselves shareholders the likelihood of them becoming aware of the contents is very high, particularly as the documents will be accessible online.

Care therefore has to be exercised in making statements in these documents, say, to the effect that employees of the organization are its 'most valuable asset'. Sadly, the employees may not recognize this to be the case, and all too often the truth is closer to the view expressed by the character known as the Pointy-Haired Boss in the Dilbert cartoon strips. He admits that he was wrong to have made such an assertion, and corrects himself by saying that 'Money is our most valuable asset. Employees are ninth', before going on to explain that they come just after carbon paper in the pecking order!

The description of employees as the most valuable asset is the sort of statement that is clearly made with the best of motives, and it is in all probability a strongly held belief. Unfortunately the opportunities for it to be a statement unsupported by actions are legion, with a resultant cynicism and loss of trust amongst employees.

Television, press and other media

All too often, employees first learn about significant developments by reading press articles, watching the news on television or browsing on the web. Where the organization concerned is a company, and is bound by local stock exchange regulations requiring it to inform the stock market on which it is listed before anyone else, it can be an insuperable problem to inform employees ahead of such an announcement. The relevant authorities take a dim view of such information being leaked and not delivered through the appropriate channels.

However, there are occasions when employees learn indirectly about developments that are not likely to affect the company's share price, and the effect can be demotivating, particularly as the reporting may not fully reflect all of the relevant information, yet the report will still colour perceptions of any subsequent official communication.

Again to illustrate the antithesis of how such matters should be handled we have to look no further than another of the inspired Dilbert cartoons of Scott Adams. In this one the Pointy-Haired Boss is talking to the HR director. One says to the other, 'We need to tell our employees about the merger,' to which the reply is, 'They'll read it in the news. Why should we do the extra work?'

Employees have a very reasonable expectation of being informed about developments that affect their company and their job ahead of anyone else, and ideally would like to be given this information in person by their superiors.

EMPLOYEE RESEARCH

The use of market research techniques and approaches is primarily about gaining the views of the workforce, and as such may not appear to be much concerned with the flow of information to the workforce. Yet irrespective of which research methodology may be in use at any one time, the way in which the workforce is informed about the research, how they are invited to take part, along with the subject matter of the research, and any actions that ensue from it will all be saying something to the recipients about how the organization views them and the topics under discussion. As a consequence it becomes another form of communication to the workforce, who can be motivated or demotivated by it according to their perception of the exercise.

CONCLUSIONS

Although this chapter is not an exhaustive catalogue of the ways in which communication takes place, it nevertheless is a demonstration of the variety available. The permutations and combinations of media deployed at any one time need to be managed to maximum effect in order to achieve the goal of a uniform understanding across the workforce.

In addition to offering an independent and objective means of collating the views and opinions of employees, which complements other channels, research studies can inform both communication strategy and tactics. At the strategic level research can, for instance, provide inputs about what needs to be communicated, while tactically it can assist with the selection of the most appropriate media and the way in which the chosen messages might best be presented. Subsequently research can be used to follow up these communications to gauge their effectiveness, say, by assessing awareness or monitoring any changes in behaviours.

5 Good practice in setting up a survey

INTRODUCTION

Once it has been determined that some form of research is required there are many possibilities for what can be done. This chapter therefore goes through the prerequisites for, and the various stages of, a successful survey. In the process the emphasis is explicitly on those studies designed to generate output in the form of numbers (that is, quantitative research). Chapter 7 examines the requirements for and benefits of conducting qualitative research.

PREREQUISITES

It is critical to be absolutely clear on the specific objectives for the research. Not only will this lead to the identification of the optimal means of collecting the required information, it will assist with the task of gaining support for the exercise and ultimately the implementation of actions generated by the feedback gained.

Sometimes surveys are conducted for reasons that may make sense to the person commissioning the research, but if the logic is not compelling to others in the organization the exercise is doomed to failure and could even be counter-productive. Occasionally a survey will set out to gather data that is not relevant or of interest to those being asked to participate, with the probable consequence that they will not respond. Indeed, if it is seen as an opportunity missed to gather meaningful feedback, employees may even feel demotivated by what they perceive to be a lack of interest on the part of the organization.

Where these situations arise they can reflect emotions such as fear on the part of those commissioning the study: fear of what they will actually learn should they ask the 'right' questions. Alternatively they can be guilty of excessive pride in believing that they know what the issues should be and what the answers are. Whatever the reasoning, there are clear dangers that the effectiveness of the study will be undermined if the agenda of the person commissioning it is not in tune with the needs or wants of the people being asked the questions.

As importantly, and probably more pertinent to employee research than any other type of research, there must be a commitment by the management of the organization to act on the findings. This in turn will lead to a greater involvement amongst employees. While low survey response rates can be a function of various factors (such as perceived lack of confidentiality or poor survey design), significant among them will be previous failures to provide honest feedback on the results or to provide a statement of what action will be taken.

WRITING A RESEARCH BRIEF

Whether or not an external agency is employed in such projects (the benefits of using one are examined later), it is extremely useful to write a briefing document that contains all of the relevant information that would be helpful to anyone who is going to be involved as a potential supplier, a coordinator or even a respondent.

The brief should start by setting out the background to the proposed study, providing the wider context in which the research is to take place. This will involve saying something about the organization, its structure and its ambitions, for the benefit of any external parties.

This opening section then naturally leads on to a statement of the broad objectives for, and specific requirements of, the research that is being proposed. The importance of clarity and consensus here is best demonstrated at the completion of any study, as it provides the standard against which it is possible to gauge whether the research has provided the information that was needed. Sometimes the research equivalent of 'mission creep' can occur, whereby the study ends up answering a different set of issues from those originally envisaged.

In addition, notably where there is an array of parties involved in setting up the study, there can be several agendas and so a realistic aggregation of requirements is essential to avoid trying to provide answers to every conceivable question. When surveys are too long, and occasionally ask unanswerable questions, the net effect is that few people will be tempted to complete them and so there will be little by way of usable data.

As well as defining the primary objectives of the study, a brief should also set out how the results will be used. This helps to clarify the objectives as well as giving some direction to the way in which the results are to be presented. The brief may also give guidance on the proposed scope of the project, including the number, types and geographical spread of employees to be involved in the research. Furthermore it is helpful to include a schedule of key timings or dates such as a target date for the production, and communication, of research results.

Setting out the parameters in this way means that all interested parties, including the management team, can comment on and subsequently endorse an approach which will require the commitment of all for it to be a success. After it has been agreed, the brief can also provide the blueprint for communications to line managers, who need to be involved early in the process as their support is often vital in achieving a positive reception for the survey and its findings.

The document can then be used to brief external agencies or consultancies, where such assistance is required. In these circumstances it is helpful to provide additional information, for instance about the available budget for the research. Providing this information ensures that the competing proposals or tenders will be more easily comparable, and makes the decision which to select more straightforward. Given that external suppliers are not normally reimbursed for the costs of submitting proposals, it is usual to approach no more than four for any single project.

RESEARCH OBJECTIVES

Although the objectives for the research will be determined by the overall rationale for it, as discussed in the previous chapters, it is worth stressing the choice between two broad perspectives: information gathering and communication.

The role of employee research can be seen simply as information gathering. Alternatively, it can be seen as information exchange and communication. There is a fundamental difference between these two views. The first tends to limit the role of research to a one-way flow of information from employees to management. The second takes a broader view, defining employee research as a continuous, two-way flow of information between employees and management. This places employee research within the broader context of internal communications, and can help to raise response rates by making employees feel included in the process.

In the context of the 'information' model of employee research, objectives tend to be stated solely in terms of information requirements. The 'communication' model demands consideration of wider questions, such as how the information is going to be acted on by management and how these actions are going to be communicated back to employees. Additionally there are matters of implementation: such as the extent to which employees will be involved in responding to the problems and opportunities that the research raises, or how the implementation of these actions will be monitored over time.

Quite often the intention will be to keep the channel of communication open between employees and management. If so, the way in which it is intended to be handled will need to be set out. All these additional questions will help focus the research on those areas in which the company is committed to making real improvements, and help manage the longer-term effects that research can have on an organization and its employees.

THE ADVANTAGES OF USING AN EXTERNAL SUPPLIER

While organizations may conduct their own employee research in-house, typically in the expectation of reducing costs, there are various benefits to be gained from using external suppliers. There is a considerable variety in the type of agency and consultancy claiming to offer expertise in employee research. The particular benefit attached to using agencies and consultants affiliated to the Market Research Society is that they are backed by the Code of Conduct, which was designed to support and maintain professional standards (see Appendix 2). Adherence to this Code of Conduct also ensures that research is conducted in accordance with the principles of the Data Protection Act.

More generally there are a number of benefits to be derived from using external suppliers rather than in-house resources, and the main ones are considered in this section.

Independence

When someone is engaged by an organization solely for the purposes of gathering the views of employees he or she will not be party to the internal 'political' pressures that exist within all organizations. The benefit here is twofold. First, the perceived lack of bias will encourage full participation by employees. This is particularly important when an organization is conducting such research for the first time and there is no culture of participating in this type of study.

Without a reference point based on prior experience, employees can be suspicious about what will happen to any views they express or information they provide. Hence there is a great value in being able to demonstrate quite readily that the researcher has no desire to (indeed, has a professional obligation not to) abuse the confidence in which the information and views have been given.

The second benefit is that there is no vested interest on the part of the researchers at the reporting stage. Again their professional integrity requires them to report fully and accurately on the views of the employees, and there is no reason for them to do otherwise. In contrast, an employee of the organization inevitably has links and associations with various parts of the organization, and so the temptation can arise, for instance, to be selective in the way results are reported: possibly filtering out results that reflect poorly on certain parts of the organization.

Resources

Programmes of research, particularly attitude surveys involving a census of staff views, can put a great deal of strain on internal resources. Indeed, such surveys often take place when the organization is already under pressure, if it is in transition and undergoing a major change programme. Using an external agency can reduce this additional burden on resources and allow the company to concentrate on its core activities.

This benefit will be especially felt where the organization has limited or possibly zero experience of conducting such research. However, it is rare for an organization to outsource the entire operation of a survey; indeed internal ownership is frequently marked by the establishment of a network of coordinators charged with the responsibility for the successful implementation of the survey in their area. Such a network will benefit from training in these additional responsibilities, and this training can usefully be administered by experienced personnel provided by the external supplier.

Large-scale surveys, particularly those conducted using paper questionnaires, and to a lesser extent those conducted by phone or online, are heavy on administration, as for instance it is vital that everyone who is expected to take part is given, and seen to be given, the opportunity to participate. The situation to avoid is one where individuals are not able to take part purely as a result of poor administration, yet it is obvious to them that all of their colleagues are participating in the study.

Expertise

In addition to providing resources in terms of people to handle certain aspects of a survey, external research specialists can also draw on their specific expertise of conducting such surveys. This expertise can range from designing the most suitable research methodology for the organization through to interpreting the results. Along the way it could involve the translation of the questionnaire into different languages or dialects, as well as the technical resource to set up and run an online survey.

Some suppliers offer the opportunity to compare results with other companies, providing a wider context for the interpretation of research findings. In turn this can lead to the provision of opportunities to share best practice with other clients the supplier has worked with.

Anonymity and confidentiality

One of the major facets underpinning the MRS Code of Conduct has been the protection of the anonymity of respondents in any market research study. Occasionally, the respondents may wish for the end-client of a study to know that it was them who made a particular contribution: for example, if a customer has a dispute with a company that needs to be resolved. In such circumstances if, and only if, the respondent provides explicit permission for his or her details to be divulged will the anonymity of the response be removed.

For employee surveys, anonymity is further strengthened by a provision limiting the reporting of the results for a unit to those units where a minimum number of 10 people take part. Without such a safeguard, in a situation, say, where there were only five respondents, it might be possible for someone in the organization to identify a given individual from the pattern of responses, with the effect of compromising that individual's anonymity.

NEXT STEPS IN CONDUCTING A QUANTITATIVE STUDY

Up to this point, the guidance in this chapter is more or less equally as applicable to qualitative research as it is to quantitative, since both benefit from a clarity of objectives, a commitment to action, guarantees of anonymity for participants and so on. Indeed, the issues of resources and expertise are probably even more critical in the case of qualitative research, as it requires a skill set that is less likely to be found outside a company that specializes in research.

From this point the chapter will assume that the decision has been made in favour of a quantitative study (as opposed to one involving qualitative research techniques) reflecting the need for numerical measurements. This in turn invokes the use of statistical analysis of the answers and enables direct comparisons between sets of data (for example between groups of people and points in time). Almost by definition, quantitative research offers an approach best suited to covering large groups of people.

The remainder of this section now considers the next steps that undertaking a quantitative study will entail, starting with the all-important questionnaire.

Drawing up the questionnaire

A number of factors need to be considered when deciding on questionnaire wording and content. First and foremost will be the specific information objectives of the research, since any failure to address these will mean an opportunity missed and possibly a commitment broken. Occasionally the list of objectives can be over-long, with the consequence that doing justice to them all results in a questionnaire that is itself excessively long. In this situation an examination of all the objectives is required, and some ordering of priorities so that agreement can be obtained to a shortened list from all the parties concerned.

Previous sections have mentioned the need to reconcile the agendas of those responsible for the study and those completing the questionnaires. The inputs from the latter are most readily available if there have been similar studies conducted previously, in which respondents were able to comment on the questionnaire itself. Alternatively, research can be undertaken specifically to obtain these inputs. Research of this type is likely to be qualitative in nature so that the issues can be explored in depth, and is most beneficial when a quantitative study is being planned for the first time and the organization has a 'blank sheet of paper' for a questionnaire. Such research must also be distinguished from a pilot study (see later), which is normally conducted on a smaller scale with a questionnaire that simply needs to be fine-tuned.

As more organizations use research methods to gather the views of employees, the more likely it is that any one organization will have existing research to draw upon in its efforts to decide upon the content of a fresh study. Specifically where the organization is planning a further survey of a similar nature to those conducted previously, it will be faced by the need to balance keeping the questionnaire consistent with those used in the past and updating it for any changing circumstances. In practice, both aims need to be met as there is little point in pretending that the world has not changed or that there are not new and different priorities. Equally, in order to track the views of employees in a way that permits robust comparisons over time, it is critical that there is consistency in the line of questioning.

The next consideration concerns the desire for some form of external benchmarking. A previous chapter considered the principal merits of this as an approach to or reason for conducting a survey. In addition to these points there is the matter of how it relates specifically to the construction of a questionnaire. The database of questions that the external suppliers have should be full of those that are tried and tested and devoid of any ambiguities. Assuming that the questions cover the ground the organization is interested in, it can make sense to use a form of wording that has proved successful elsewhere, irrespective of whether the data from other organizations is going to be available and comparisons made.

Different types of question

When drawing up a questionnaire there are certain types of question that offer specific benefits in maximizing the value to be derived from the study. It is not the intention here to offer comprehensive advice on writing questionnaires as that warrants an entire book in its own right. Indeed, readers are encouraged to turn to Ian Brace's authoritative *Questionnaire Design* (2004). This section instead concentrates on some issues relevant to lines of questioning that appear in employee opinion surveys.

Closed and open questions

The simplest form of closed question is one to which the respondent is invited to answer either 'yes' or 'no'. This form plays a role in employee opinion surveys, notably in connection with factual elements: for example, 'Have you attended a training course in the last year?' More common in such surveys however is the type of question inviting respondents to choose one of a number of ratings from a scale.

For example, presented with a statement such as 'My manager listens to new ideas and suggestions,' respondents might be asked to select one of the following options: agree strongly, agree, neither agree nor disagree, disagree, disagree strongly. This type of question, which is closed in the sense that there are a given number of options for a response, is discussed in more detail below.

By contrast, an open question on this topic, in which respondents are given complete freedom to answer in any way they liked, could be phrased as follows: 'How does your manager respond to new ideas and suggestions?' The breadth of possible answers is such that it is more difficult to aggregate the responses from a large number of employees, in contrast to the common currency of the agree/disagree scale present in the closed alternative. So using a closed question with a predetermined scale of answers has the benefit of simplifying the process while also providing a basis of consistency across groups of employees.

Open questions tend to be used more in surveys that are administered by an interviewer. Here uses can include asking for a spontaneous or top-of-mind reaction; or as a follow-up question exploring a previous answer in more depth. Since many employee studies involve respondents completing the questionnaire themselves, there tends to be less usage of open questions. Without the prompting of an interviewer, most respondents will not go into much detail. Moreover, a self-completion questionnaire is not conducive to asking the equivalent questions to those frequently seen in interviewer-led consumer research, such as the spontaneous recall of a brand name or a product attribute. With a self-completion questionnaire there is the danger that the 'answers' will be mentioned elsewhere, prompting respondents with potential answers that they might not have given spontaneously.

The most common use of an open question in employee research is at the conclusion of a questionnaire. This generally allows respondents the opportunity to comment on any aspect of working life in the organization. Apart from anything else, it represents a very important safety valve that caters for any aspects not covered elsewhere in the study.

Questions using verbal rating scales

The example above with an agree/disagree scale is of a form of questioning referred to as a Likert scale, after Rensis Likert who first described it in 1932. Typically there are the five points on the scale, although it is not unknown to use seven points (adding agree/disagree very strongly to either end). In theory, having more points in the scale means that greater discrimination can be extracted from the answers, although if the end points are too exacting there is little likelihood that anyone will select them.

Frequently respondents are invited to give reactions to statements using other types of rating scales, which range from, say, very effective to not very effective; very good to very poor; a lot to a little; one of the best to one of the worst; or very committed to not at all committed. The key requirement is to match the rating scale to the statement. It is unlikely to make sense to people if, say, they are asked to use a scale from very satisfied to very dissatisfied when responding to the statement 'I am adequately trained to do my job'.

Varying the rating scales gives the additional benefit of breaking up the questionnaire and making it more interesting to complete. Where a questionnaire occupies several pages in the same format and layout, respondents can find it tedious and fall into a pattern of responses (such as always ticking the left-hand column) which does not reflect their true feelings.

Occasionally there is debate about the freedom respondents should be granted to be non-committal in their answers. The option of 'neither agree nor disagree' can be a legitimate answer, as people may not have a strong opinion one way or the other. It is also used on occasion to allow respondents the option of 'don't know', although it is probably better if the design presents that as a separate option. If the neutral/don't know options are removed the respondent is forced to express a view one way or the other.

However, if the requirement is to measure those expressing a positive opinion (whether it is those agreeing with a positively worded statement like 'Everyone gets on well in this office' or disagreeing with one that is negatively worded like 'Morale here is poor'), the need can be met by the way the information is reported. So it may be more appropriate to give respondents the full range of options and simply report the percentages who express a positive opinion. Indeed, just such an approach has become something of a standard way to reduce large amounts of data from such surveys down to key indicators.

The differences between 'me, we, (s)he and they'

When a statement is included in a questionnaire, it can be phrased in a variety of ways including:

- first person singular ('I am motivated to perform to a high level');
- first person plural ('People in this department are motivated to perform to a high level');
- third person singular ('Our manager motivates us to perform to a high level');
- third person plural ('The company motivates us to perform to a high level').

Apart from any difficulties connected with comparing results over time or between organizations when different statements appearing to cover the same topic have been used, it is important to consider how the same individual may respond to each type of statement.

If the question is phrased personally, an individual is much more likely to give an 'acceptable' or positive answer – for example, to say that he or she is personally well motivated – because a negative answer would reflect poorly on the individual as well as on those people involved in motivating him or her. (This is not simply about motivation, as it could apply to a statement about communication or training or anything else.)

In contrast, a 'we' statement such as the second one above gives the respondent licence to admit that, while he or she may be well motivated, there are several other people in the department who are not. The third statement introduces an extra dimension with the involvement of a third party, in this case the manager. However intrinsically motivated the group of individuals in the department may be, the manager can of course have an enormous impact, either positively or negatively.

The last statement takes matters one further step by talking about the company in more general terms. This then becomes a comment on the senior management and the ethos of the organization, and it is much less likely that, by being inevitably removed from the day-to-day life of the respondent, senior management will be seen as having a significant role in motivating employees.

There is therefore plenty of scope for apparently similarly worded statements to generate a diverse range of responses even from one respondent. While the selection of the particular form of question will depend on the objectives of the study, it is clearly important to be consistent in the form used across surveys and groups of similar questions in any one survey. Otherwise it will only be possible to make superficial comparisons between surveys where different forms of a statement have been used.

Designing the questionnaire

The appearance and layout of questionnaires can have a major influence on both the response rate and the accuracy of results. Opinions differ over whether question formats should be kept consistent throughout, to speed completion and minimize confusion about what is required, or varied in style in order to hold the interest of respondents. As mentioned above, excessive consistency in the form of long lists of questions using the same scales can lead to boredom, as well as the danger that respondents will follow a pattern in their answers.

It is of course desirable to get respondents to think about the answers they are giving. This can be achieved by breaking up question areas into short sections and by varying the scales used for the answers. Within a short section it is also possible to vary the line of questioning by mixing up positively and negatively worded statements. In contrast, inserting a negative statement in a long list of positively worded statements runs the risk that the respondent will read it as a positive one and give an answer opposite to the one intended.

Another rationale for mixing positively and negatively worded questions, in addition to getting respondents to stop and think about their answers, is that it allows an element of checking on the consistency in the views they express. While this has some merit, it is important to limit the number of times this is done in the same questionnaire, as it will become evident to respondents that the author of the questionnaire is more concerned with verifying their responses than ascertaining their views. Again the consequence of this perception will be that many respondents will decline to complete the task.

A further consideration in the presentation of a questionnaire is the use of graphics, and particularly logos and branding. Some organizations specifically develop branding of their employee surveys as part of the reinforcement process, to aid identification of related communication materials and to build the engagement with the process.

Overall, a questionnaire that is attractively presented, with the questions split into meaningful sections and asked in a way that is relevant to respondents, will contribute significantly to a successful study. And the best way of assessing whether this is the case in advance is to pilot the questionnaire.

Piloting the questionnaire

Once the questionnaire has been developed, it is essential to test it amongst a cross-section of employees to ensure that it is user-friendly, and that all the questions are comprehensible, unambiguous and relevant. A pilot exercise will normally involve a qualitative approach as it will be more beneficial to obtain thoughts about the questions that work and are relevant, the questions that are neither of these things, as well as any questions that should be included but are not in the draft.

CASE STUDY

Cadbury Schweppes wished to adopt common systems and processes throughout all of its subsidiary companies across Great Britain and Ireland. One business unit was chosen as the location for the initial implementation phase. There was therefore a clear intention to learn lessons from this one site before rolling out the systems and processes to the rest of the region, and subsequently the other companies in the group.

The nature and the scale of the changes was guaranteed to touch all employees through quicker and improved decision making, improved processes, data flows and management information, leading to more rewarding and fulfilling roles for the employees in the business. Since the changes were to the systems and processes, there was also going to be a lot of data generated, from which the success of the exercise could be determined.

The one area of information that would not be delivered automatically related to the employees themselves. In particular it was important to find out whether the changes were actually making their jobs more rewarding and fulfilling, and if they were realizing the benefits that were meant to accrue to them.

The situation was therefore one where it was going to be important to devise a means of obtaining feedback from all employees. It was also intended that regular measures would be taken over time, with the first coming fairly soon after implementation so that employees could still accurately recall what their job had been like before the changes.

Given that there was no history or experience to draw on it was especially important that the development of the questionnaire for this survey included a pilot stage to check that it was covering the correct areas in the right manner. A series of individual interviews and a group discussion, drawing on a cross-section of employees, were used to find out how people felt about the changes and to take them through a first draft of the questionnaire. The strength and uniformity of the views persuaded the management team to defer consulting through a wider study until a later date.

This was the reasoning behind the decision. While employees could see the benefits of the changes that would ultimately accrue, in the immediate post-implementation phase their workloads involved were temporarily very high. The concerns this created were therefore likely to colour any views gathered at this stage. By undertaking a quantitative study, and acting on reported concerns across the workforce at this stage, the management team would in effect be taking a false reading. They would therefore be in danger in making unnecessary corrective action when the views of the employees would in due course return to equilibrium as new working patterns settled down.

Piloting of the questionnaire is also extremely important in an international study, when the questionnaire has to be translated into different languages. The pilot will allow for the identification and correction of differences in idiom and dialect which may not be familiar to the person designing or translating the questionnaire.

Employees can rightly be demanding of the standard of the communications that they receive from the organization they work for. Particularly in the case of a self-completion questionnaire, with no interviewer intervention to correct the language used, any uncorrected errors will be very visible.

Questionnaire completion

There are two main types of data collection method used in employee research: interviewer-administered (either face to face or by telephone) and self-completion (whether individually or in groups, and either on paper or screen).

Interviewer-administered questionnaires

While many consumers are taken through research questionnaires by an interviewer, in employee research the most common method used is self-completion. The main benefits of this approach are speed and cost-effectiveness.

However, there is little point in spending less money if the information yield is very low. Consequently, it can represent a good return on the investment to use interviewers. This could be the case, for example, in those situations where it is important to gain an immediate or sponta-neous response to particular issues, or there is a need to use a complicated form of questioning that cannot easily be catered for in a self-completion questionnaire.

Trained interviewers are also particularly good at probing responses and eliciting a deeper understanding of the reasons respondents feel as they do about particular issues. Less common, but occasionally impor-tant, is the need to involve interviewers when elements of the workforce may have problems with literacy or language, necessitating assistance in the survey process.

In most cases interviewers tend to be used only when the number of employees involved in the research is relatively small. Again, this is largely an issue of economics, given the cost of employing an interviewing field force large enough to cover all respondents in a substantial organi-zation. The economics are slightly improved when the interviewing is conducted over the phone.

Irrespective of the cost and time implications of using interviewers, it is also important to decide how these interviewers will be 'positioned': as part of the organization or part of an independent third party. Apart from the considerations about employing an independent agency set out above, there is a further specific consideration of how it may affect the responses.

Quite simply, although employees can sometimes be critical of the organization they work for, they will tend to be less so when discussing the matter externally. Comparable surveys have shown that when inter-views are deemed to be 'within the family' (that is, conducted by internal interviewers) responses will be more critical than when the same ques-tions are asked by external interviewers. Similar behaviours can be ob-served outside a research context, when otherwise critical employees can become strong advocates when their employer is criticized by someone else.

Self-completion questionnaires

Traditionally, self-completion questionnaires have been paper-based. There are a number of ways in which they can be distributed: by line managers (preferably accompanied by an explanatory briefing), by internal mail, or even direct to employees' home addresses. This flexibility is important where the workforce is widely dispersed and increasing numbers do not have a permanent work base: for example, with a peripatetic sales force or the expanding numbers of workers basing themselves at home.

Where the distribution of employees and the nature of their work make it possible, group self-completion can be very successful in achieving a higher response rate. An example of the sort of location where this can take place is a canteen outside meal times. Employees are invited to attend on a phased basis so that each has sufficient space and time to complete his or her own questionnaire. Setting aside time during working hours to complete the task demonstrates to employees that the company takes the survey seriously. It can also help to shorten the elapsed time between distributing and collecting the completed questionnaires.

The importance of self-completion surveys in the conduct of employee surveys has meant that the advent of e-mail and internet technology was always likely to have a significant impact. For this reason, the use of these electronic methods of undertaking studies is considered in a separate chapter (Chapter 6).

Census or sample?

There are good arguments for conducting a census of all employees when undertaking company-wide surveys. It demonstrates that the company is interested in everyone's views, avoids any problems concerning non-inclusion, and allows the production of actionable reports at localized levels. There are circumstances, however, where some form of selection (or sampling) may be sensible.

It can simply be the case that an organization is so vast, with employees numbered in hundreds of thousands, that it is impractical to address everyone at once. Here the solution is more likely to lie in conducting surveys within divisions or subsidiaries than genuine sampling across the entire organization. However, true sampling has a role to play when surveys are being repeated on a regular basis to track changing perspectives over time. Here it would be detrimental to continued participation if all staff were asked for their views too often without seeing any direct benefit. In addition, the whole purpose of sampling from a statistical perspective is to replicate the views of the population without the need (and by implication the effort and expense) to ask everyone.

When a sampling approach has been chosen, selection should be arranged to ensure that each sample represents a balanced cross-section of the whole to avoid skewed or unrepresentative data. This can be achieved either by drawing a random sample or by setting quotas (a representative proportion of the whole according to sub-groups such as department, job grade, age, working locations). The latter is the more common method. Genuine random sampling requires the generation of a set of random numbers which are then used to select those asked to participate. In practice it is more common to selecting every nth name from an alphabetical list of employees.

CASE STUDY

When the retail bank NatWest chose to embark on a major cultural change programme across the entire organization, it deployed a range of communications media in support. Following on from various launch events around the country, the impetus was to be maintained through regular team briefings, videos and internal publications. There was therefore a need to track progress towards the goal of a transformation to a customer and results-oriented organization.

A sampling approach was therefore taken so that individual employees were only occasionally asked to take part, limiting the scope for research fatigue. Equally importantly, the research, which was conducted by telephone (to maximize the value of some open-ended questions and ensure that the questioning went deeper and probed whether real change had taken place) could take place without raising expectations of actions at each and every survey period, when it was primarily a vehicle for monitoring progress.

Communicating the survey

Prior publicity is important to ensuring high rates of response. Any number of media can be deployed to advise employees of the survey and its purpose, ranging from in-house magazines to videos and posters as well as e-mail and the intranet. It is recommended that this is reinforced with face-to-face briefings from line managers at the time the survey is distributed.

Additionally, a letter from the chief executive (or other relevant person with authority) sent prior to the survey, or accompanying the questionnaire, can be very influential. This should signal the commitment of senior management both to the survey process and to acting on the results of the research.

As well as communication with employees at the outset, there should be continuing communication throughout the research programme. Regular updates will not only inform employees of progress and maintain interest levels, they can also act as a reminder to those who have still to take part either because they have been away or simply not got around to it.

Ensuring high response rates

As with the turn-out in a democratic election, it is self-evidently a good thing that as many employees as possible take part in any study in which they are asked to participate. Where the response rate is low, the management of the organization will have more difficulty determining the view of the workforce as a whole.

Beyond this, a study by Rogelberg *et al* (2000) demonstrated that employees who do not respond to surveys are less satisfied and more likely to resign than are employees who respond to attitude surveys. The results of this study, in conjunction with previous research, indicate that employers should view a lack of complaints or a low response rate as a sign of trouble rather than a sign that everything is going well. It is potentially a situation where no news cannot be said to be good news.

Response rates can be affected by a number of factors which may be difficult to influence because their origins lie elsewhere, such as general levels of motivation in, and commitment to, the company. However, there are steps that can be taken to improve rates of response, most of which have been touched upon in previous sections. These include the merits of publicizing the survey in advance, and ensuring that line managers are well briefed, so that the importance of completing the survey is reinforced among their staff. Thereafter it should help if response rates are publicized during the survey completion period and a local system of survey coordinators is arranged to encourage participation.

It will further assist if employees are assured of the survey's confidentiality and the questionnaire has been piloted to ensure that it is relevant and user-friendly. Employees may also be persuaded to take part if the time is provided during working hours for completion of the questionnaire. Even where this is done, it is normally good practice to allow a period for completion of about three weeks, so that anyone who is away for reasons such as holiday, a business trip or short-term sickness still has the opportunity to take part on their return.

Generally in research there are debates about the merits of, and the need for, incentivizing potential respondents by offering a tangible (typically monetary) reward. In the case of employee research, especially given the hope that employees are engaged in a dialogue, there is less reason to think in these terms.

The very closeness of the relationship between employer and employee means that there should be much more direct benefit to an employee arising from participating than is ever likely to be the case in research among customers. Indeed, rewarding individuals or groups directly on the basis of response rates is open to abuse, with those who genuinely do not wish to take part coming under undue pressure to do so. In some circumstances it may be appropriate to acknowledge a high level of response in a particular office or division, but the beneficiary should be a third party such as a charity.

Interest in the subject matter contained in the questionnaire is a very strong motivator to take part. A good example comes from a bank that wished to explore the attitudes of managers to the company car scheme. The study took place at a time when paper-based surveys were more common, and a sample of managers in the bank was sent a questionnaire printed on blue paper. The response exceeded 100 per cent. Those who were sent the questionnaire were motivated to respond by a subject that aroused stronger emotions than most. On top of this some of their colleagues who did not receive a questionnaire, found out about it and took copies in order to submit their views. Unfortunately for them copiers contained white paper, so it was very easy to distinguish the responses that were solicited from those that were unsolicited.

Finally, one of the most common and certainly the most telling reasons for employees not completing a questionnaire is the belief that nothing will change as a result of the survey. If response rates are low, ensuring that some form of well-publicized action follows the survey will rekindle interest in the process and result in an increased rate of response when the survey is repeated.

Analysing and reporting the results

Once the deadline for completion of the survey has passed, with the possible addition of a period of grace to allow for any submissions arriving by post, the in-house project team or external agency (as appropriate) has the responsibility of collating all the answers. This will then enable them to provide their clients with the outputs or deliverables that have been agreed upon. Typically these consist of a report containing statistical tables and a graphical presentation of key sets of data, along with a commentary on the findings and a management summary. The report and particularly the graphics are frequently presented using the traffic light style. Disappointing results will be presented in red, encouraging results in green and anything else in orange or yellow.

While the 'total' results from a company-wide survey may be of great interest to senior managers and the HR department, most people's interest will tend to be limited to their local region, department or business unit. If the results are to have an effect on the company at a local level, this localized data must be supplied. The only limit on this form of sub-analysis is confidentiality. A lower limit of 10 respondents for any sub-group should be agreed to ensure that no individual employee's views can be identified.

However, it will be the responsibility of the organization's management to add to this local data some reactions and thoughts about how any of the issues raised in the research will be addressed. Subsequently, further reports should be distributed updating employees on progress with these action items.

Local action planning

Increasingly, companies involve employees in formulating local plans of action in response to the survey results. This activity can usually be facilitated by local managers, with support and guidance from the research project team. To ensure that the communications loop is complete, resultant action plans are typically circulated to more senior managers, both for their information and to gain appropriate authorization for local decisions.

CASE STUDY

Manpower is a leading provider of employment services, and the group is comfortably in the top 200 of *Fortune*'s list of US companies and the top 500 globally, with an annual turnover in 2004 of almost US $15 billion. Apart from the parent brand, the company is made up of other well-known specialist providers such as Brook Street, Elan, Jefferson Wells and Right Management Consultants. It is therefore a real people business, which prides itself on its commitment to employees and customers.

One of the things that has characterized the growth of the organization is the entrepreneurial spirit whereby as well as growing by acquisition (hence the range of brands) Manpower has also grown organically by encouraging individuals to establish new businesses in different territories. As an example, the biggest marketplace for the group is now France rather than the United States.

One of the consequences of this growth pattern has been that the individual country managers inevitably have a lot of autonomy. In addition the main form of group-wide communication tended to relate to financial and business performance. Jeff Joerres, who was appointed as CEO and President in 1999, saw the opportunity of an employee survey to drive a global culture and to

---

encourage people at all levels to communicate upwards. This latter aspect is given an additional importance as the structure of the mainstream businesses often revolves around offices with a small number of employees and little of a hierarchy between them and the country managers, so there are not the channels for communication that are seen in other large organizations.

The survey, entitled the Annual People Survey, run by Right Management Consultants on behalf of the group, has now evolved such that in its third year (2004) it encompassed all 27,000 employees in the group and was conducted online. Although not all staff have their own PC, those who do not received a paper invitation to participate using a dedicated terminal, and everyone was given a unique link as a security measure and to avoid any abuse such as completing multiple responses. The geographical coverage of the group necessitated the translation of the questionnaire, to which local survey coordinators could add their own questions, into 26 languages.

Among the various uses of the data, a rating for 'engagement' was devised, which was planned to be incorporated into balanced business scorecards and used to determine an element of the compensation for senior executives. This rating is simple to calculate and easily understood: it is the proportion of employees in a chosen area who respond positively to all four key measures of satisfaction, motivation, employer advocacy and service/brand advocacy.

To ensure that all of the results are fully utilized, the group has an eight-step plan for effective action planning. This starts with country managers reviewing the results and then communicating the findings to all employees. In doing this the managers are charged with identifying three priority areas that need to be addressed. These priority areas are then explored in detail so that effective solutions can be formulated, before the managers sign off the preferred courses of action. These decisions can then be communicated to all staff before the detailed planning takes places. Thereafter the implementation is subject to three-monthly reviews.

Survey frequency

In addition to providing a regular communication channel between employees and their managers, repeating surveys on a regular basis allows the company to build up an accurate picture of how the organization is developing over time. This is especially useful when goals are set and monitored in relation to key indicators such as employee satisfaction, teamwork, communication and leadership.

As part of a two-way communication process, the main determinant of survey frequency should be the amount of time it takes for the results to be reported and acted on, and for any resulting benefits to be felt. It is also important for the different types of survey that may be taking place throughout an organization to be coordinated centrally to avoid survey fatigue or redundancy. In addition, major employee surveys need to fit in with the business cycle of the organization. This needs to be taken into account at the planning stage.

QUANTITATIVE STUDIES GENERALLY

As noted previously, quantitative research techniques can be applied to much more than the wide-ranging, traditional attitude/opinion survey. Yet the latter has to be accompanied by the disciplines set out above because of its prominence, and the fact than it represents a form of communication to employees in its own right. By demonstrating how employees and their views are valued it can be a powerful means of motivating and energizing the workforce. Alternatively, if handled badly it can have the opposite effect from that intended.

A one-off study involving a smaller sample of employees on a specific subject inevitably does not have the same impact or carry the same levels of risk and reward to the organization. Yet increasingly samples of employees are being asked for their views on matters such as customer-related issues, product development, communications effectiveness and much more, and the results feed into business decision making just as the customer equivalent does.

The fact that these studies are likely to be more immediate and focused does not mean that many of the principles of conducting employee research laid out above do not apply. While it is unlikely to be necessary to communicate to all staff prior to, during and after an ad hoc study, it is still essential to have a clear project plan setting out agreed objectives, scope, the resources required and so on. For those employees invited to participate it will also still be important to communicate what the study is about, what is expected from them and how the information will be used.

There is a natural appetite among those involved in such studies, as with any other, to learn what the collective findings were, along with the decisions made on the basis of that information. It is therefore good practice to provide a summary covering these points to those who participated. Subsequently all their colleagues may be informed as part of the normal pattern of internal communications when new initiatives and developments are reported. When this happens, the simple fact that the views of employees were obtained as part of the decision-making process is a valuable message in gaining support for the changes being announced.

CONCLUSIONS

Whatever the subject matter of an employee survey, the potential benefits will only be realized with careful planning and effective communication. In part this entails having complete management support and involvement, while it is also crucial to have effective project management skills to ensure that the necessary detail is attended to.

It is also about having the requisite experience and skills so the results of any survey are used to maximum effect. For this reason it is likely that there will be benefits in drawing on research expertise from external suppliers, as few organizations conduct enough of this type of research to justify retaining people with these skills permanently.

In particular the researcher's toolkit will contain the knowledge necessary to design a meaningful questionnaire and to perform the relevant analyses that will draw out conclusions that carry weight and be of value to the organization.

6 Internet and e-mail surveys

INTRODUCTION

The impact that the internet and e-mail technology have had generally will be evident to most people. One of the areas where the technology has been deployed to great effect has been internal communications. In particular the use of e-mail and intranets have greatly assisted the flow of information to employees, and to a lesser extent opened up more opportunities for the collation of information from them.

Market research in general has seen major developments attributable to the technology, ranging from data collation through to the reporting and dissemination of results. The possibilities opened by such new developments and the benefits derived from them are considerable. Given that employee research represents a confluence of communication and research techniques, it was inevitable that the benefits brought by the technology to both should result in significant changes to the way in which employee research is conducted.

However, to avoid the risk that these developments might generate practices that are detrimental to the spirit of market research, the Market Research Society has produced some guidelines relating to internet research. These guidelines provide a useful starting point for the chapter in that they define what constitutes internet research. From this point the chapter goes on to consider the benefits of various approaches, and in particular web-based methodologies.

With the use of the technology generally, new ways of doing things should not be allowed to obscure some of the more fundamental principles involved. It can be dangerous to assume that new approaches should be adopted in every situation. The chapter therefore also examines some of the specific considerations when undertaking employee research before rounding off with the more general points as set out in the guidelines.

WHAT CONSTITUTES INTERNET RESEARCH

The MRS Guidelines on Internet Research act as a useful reminder of some of the key components of the MRS Code of Conduct as they relate to the obligations placed upon researchers when seeking the views and opinions of potential respondents. They are also very similar to the ethical guidelines published by the Marketing Research Association in the United States and ESOMAR's *Guidelines on Conducting Marketing and Opinion Research Using the Internet*.

.The guidelines start by providing a description of what constitutes internet research, and identify five categories. The first involves a respondent completing a questionnaire online via the internet regardless of access route. The second entails downloading a questionnaire from a server on the internet and returning it by e-mail. The next category deals with the receipt of a questionnaire incorporated into an e-mail and returning it in the same way.

The fourth category relates to the participation in an online qualitative interview or discussion. Finally internet research is also deemed to include taking part in a measurement system which tracks web usage using specialist software installed on the user's computer.

Although monitoring of internet usage by employees is a fact of life in many organizations and the subject of policies which have become part of the terms and conditions of employment, this last category is less relevant to the scope of this book. In addition, the use of online methods for qualitative research is considered in Chapter 7.

This chapter is therefore concerned primarily with the use of e-mail and the internet in conducting quantitative research surveys. When e-mail first became available many organizations gave employees use of internal e-mail facilities before they had access to the internet and external e-mail. At that time the internal e-mail capability assisted with the distribution and return of questionnaires. Increasingly, e-mail is used for communicating with employees about a survey rather than as a channel of distribution for questionnaires.

Before going on to consider the broader benefits of web-based surveys, it is worth looking at the specific comparison between the alternatives of an e-mail approach and one that is web-based, using either the internet or an intranet. It is also necessary to be clear about the terminology used. Although e-mail is included in the definition of internet research, since the questionnaire is not completed online it is only for the web-based media of the internet and intranets that the online description is used.

E-MAIL, AN INTRANET OR THE INTERNET?

When considering an employee survey most organizations seek to take advantage of the opportunities afforded by technology. In practice, there is still a significant role to be played by paper questionnaires given the incomplete coverage of the relevant technology across many organizations. Indeed surveys frequently use mixed methodologies to maximize coverage of and participation by employees. However, the focus of this section is on those routes that do not involve paper.

E-mail

With e-mail it is possible to advise people about a survey that is taking place, direct them to complete it online or to download a copy; or attach the questionnaire to the message itself. When e-mail is used in the latter way it represents a superior form of distributing questionnaires to employees than the physical distribution required for paper questionnaires.

Also, in contrast to a web-based survey where it may not be immediately apparent how big the questionnaire is, the use of e-mail and a questionnaire as an attachment makes it clearer to recipients how much of their time will be involved, because they can readily make an assessment of the document size.

However, using e-mail as the method of distribution for the questionnaires relies on all recipients having the relevant software, and configuration of their machines such that the questionnaire can be viewed on-screen in the manner intended by the sender. It also assumes that the attachment is suitable to pass firewalls and security barriers.

As mentioned previously, e-mail is also a prominent means of advising employees about a survey that is taking place even if the questionnaire is not attached to the message, but is to be accessed from a central server. It is of course possible to use other broadcast media to inform employees, and it is recognized that not all organizations using e-mail have a centralized database of e-mail addresses. However, increasingly the probability is that any organization contemplating running a survey like this will have e-mail addresses for all relevant employees, making it a personalized and more obvious route to go down.

The use of e-mail to communicate the details of the online survey can streamline the process, as an operational hyperlink to the relevant site can be inserted into the message so that the recipient is encouraged to visit the site immediately (rather than just directing respondents to a web address that they have to copy or type in). Without an operational hyperlink there is the possibility that the invitation will be put aside and not responded to. The hyperlink can also be combined with a password, and this brings other benefits which are discussed later.

When an employee is e-mailed a questionnaire there may be the option of returning it as a paper document (in the post or to a central collection point, much as would have been the case previously with paper questionnaires). Alternatively, the questionnaire can be completed on-screen and reattached to an e-mail so that it can be returned for collation (provided that other steps are taken such as checking for viruses). Whether questionnaires are printed off-line or returned via e-mail, the processing of all of the replies is likely to involve a third party keying in the responses before any analysis can be undertaken. This adds to the timescales before action can be taken and presentations made.

Intranets and the internet

The advantages of web-based surveys, using either the internet or an intranet, relate to the technology and the opportunities it creates. For instance it opens up the possibility of using pop-up questionnaires even if these tend to be deployed in studies that are more immediate and limited in their ambitions. If a pop-up questionnaire is too long there will be few employees who complete it there and then.

In the same way that questionnaires e-mailed as attachments may not be seen consistently by all recipients if they possess different versions of the software, the full exploitation of the capabilities available when using the internet alternative depends on respondents having compatible browsers on their PCs or laptops. This is also true of operating systems, since one member of staff who has, say, Windows 95 may see the document quite differently from another with Windows NT. In the planning stage consideration needs to be given to designing the questionnaire in keeping with the lowest common standard.

When questionnaires are completed by respondents visiting a dedicated intranet or internet site, the relevant server will have the necessary software to aggregate the responses and produce instantaneous outputs for analysis, in contrast to the e-mail alternative. There are other benefits of the web-based approach, notably relating to the design of the questionnaire, but these aspects warrant a more expansive discussion which can be found later in the chapter.

The choice between using the internet or an intranet is largely about access. There are sensitivities in some organizations about giving employees access to the worldwide web. In practice the solution can be as simple as opening up the access to the one internet site that is hosting the survey so that the benefits of it being run by an independent organization (with specialist expertise and appropriate software) are realized.

Where fewer people have access to the internet than an intranet, a decision may be taken to install survey software on an internal shared drive specifically for the purpose. This can raise a significant issue regarding the perception of anonymity and confidentiality. If there are concerns that the data for individuals will be viewed by others working in the same organization, the response rate may be adversely affected. Similarly, when employees are asked to e-mail back completed questionnaires it will be evident who they have come from, and this again may raise the question of who will see the completed surveys.

A further benefit of using an internet site to collate responses, as opposed to a company intranet, is that those employees who are not office-based (because they are peripatetic or home-based, for instance) are more likely to have access to the internet than an intranet, which is usually restricted to office-based employees. Use of the internet (rather than intranet) also allows employees the option of completing the questionnaire outside the office environment, which may be an uncomfortable location in which to complete the survey, surrounded as employees are by colleagues and managers about whom they may be asked to comment.

By directing employees to a server or website to complete a questionnaire, rather than e-mailing it directly to them, it is possible, for example through the use of passwords, to ensure that each individual only completes one return. The completion of multiple questionnaires can be a particular problem in organizations where the results of employee research are linked to performance reviews or bonuses

ADVANTAGES OF WEB-BASED SURVEYS

Simply taking the above points into account, the preferred option would appear to be a combination of e-mail as a means of communication and the internet for the completion and collation of responses. Yet, provided it is an option that is available, there are far more benefits to be gained from a web-based solution.

Questionnaire design

The fact that the questionnaire for a survey is stored on a server in a single location for respondents to access does bring potential design benefits.

Ease of amendment

For a start, the design of the questionnaire can be modified right up until the last minute before it goes live (that is, when employees are expected to start completing it). Those responsible for running the systems aspects will probably not want anyone to literally wait until the last minute, as inevitably there has to be checking and testing of the questionnaire before it goes live. Yet in contrast certainly to paper questionnaires which have to be printed and physically distributed, there is clearly much more scope to amend at a late stage.

Indeed, online questionnaires even offer the scope to include modifications during the fieldwork period. In practice this will only assist with those surveys on a more specific subject where learnings from early respondents (which can be analysed almost on a real-time basis) can be incorporated to enhance the value of the information derived from those completing the questionnaire subsequently.

Modifying the questionnaire during fieldwork does not really work for large-scale studies used to collect data about attitudes and opinions, where the aggregation of responses on a consistent basis is extremely important, especially if the entire workforce is taking part. Since most people respond immediately and it is important to coordinate the invitations to participate so that no one feels left out, there is little real scope for making changes in time for them to have an effect.

The flexibility in the design stage does however represent an opportunity to be more imaginative in the layout of a questionnaire than is possible in a more static medium. In many ways simply transferring a paper questionnaire onto screen represents a wasted opportunity. As an example of the flexibility available, consider a section that contains a number of statements respondents are asked to agree or disagree with. When a respondent expresses a strong opinion either way to one, or possibly a sequence, of these statements an additional follow-up question could be inserted to probe the reasons for such views.

In contrast an attempt to achieve something similar with a paper questionnaire requires the inclusion of follow-up questions at each statement in case either strong agreement or disagreement is expressed. If this is done there is the danger that respondents will become conditioned and avoid expressing an extreme view, since it will be clear that they have to answer more questions than if a moderate view is expressed. Moreover, the addition of follow-up questions on a paper version just in case they are required inevitably lengthens the questionnaire, possibly unnecessarily.

Routing and rotation

Where a questionnaire requires respondents to answer specific questions depending on the answers given to combinations of previous questions, the instructions in a paper questionnaire can become quite complex. In addition, there is no guarantee that the respondent will follow these instructions precisely as required. The online equivalent routes respondents straight to the specific questions based on their previous answers.

Additionally, there are benefits to be gained from rotating the order of some questions or the way in which possible answers are presented. In previous chapters concerns were raised about such things as the 'order effect' or the danger of respondents going down one side of a scale. With an online version it is clearly possible to rotate (and even randomize) the order in which questions or statements appear, unlike a paper questionnaire. And since there is not the need to squeeze as many questions onto a page as possible, the online version can break up the statements or questions so that each is presented as freshly as the last.

Layout and navigation

It would of course be possible to replicate a page of a paper questionnaire onscreen but it is preferable to minimize the amount of scrolling across or down the screen that a respondent has to do. A certain amount of this has to be allowed for since not all respondents will have the same settings on their computer or the same screen size, yet it will help if this is minimized.

Apart from limiting the number of questions that appear on each screen, another important consideration is the presentation of any scales for the respondent to select from. The combination of the question and the scale will influence how many questions can be accommodated on a screen at one time.

Space can also be saved through the use of drop-down boxes containing the range of answer options. Of interest here is the evidence cited by Brace (2004), that the order of the scale in drop-down boxes (whether starting with the positive or negative end of the scale) has no effect on the responses selected. This evidence applies to those boxes containing no more than five responses, although it is acknowledged that the order could introduce an effect where the list is longer than five.

In addition to the layout of the questions, another aspect that determines the flow of the questionnaire is the ease of navigation. If respondents are given the options to go backwards or forwards at any point (rather than relying on back/forward buttons on the browser) they will be able to move smoothly through to the end. It is also important that employees are given the opportunity to break off from completing the questionnaire, either to consider their answers or to deal with an urgent aspect of their job. This means storing their answers up to the point at which they terminate the session, and allowing them to pick up from this point when they have the opportunity to finish the exercise.

Control and clarity

With an online questionnaire it is possible to ensure that all questions are answered, by indicating to respondents that they need to supply an answer before moving on. In addition, respondents can be prevented from giving multiple answers where only one option is required. With a paper questionnaire respondents might, say, amend their answer from agree to disagree, and it might not be obvious to the person processing that questionnaire which was intended. Online, such a change of mind is immediately reflected by the over-riding of the first answer given.

The difficulties of reading some types of handwriting have also made it more difficult to accommodate in paper questionnaires either open questions or questions inviting respondents to enter numerical answers. Clearly these are difficulties that are not present when employees are keying their answers in at a screen.

Another area in which the control available within the design and structure of the online questionnaire can assist respondents is in the area of demographics and classification questions. Large organizations need to be able to identify responses for broad groupings of employees such as offices or divisions. This frequently requires employees to answer a number of questions about where they work and how they fit in to the organizational structure. Unfortunately, not everyone in the organization will be as familiar with the reporting lines as those who designed them, particularly if a recent reorganization has moved functions from one division to another. The questionnaire can therefore be set up to limit the choices presented to any one respondent based on the information he or she can readily give.

Assistance

Apart from guiding respondents in the manner in which the questionnaire is to be completed, use of the technology means that online help screens can be made available to assist with instructions on completing the questionnaire, or with definitions and explanation of terms used. For instance, look-up tables can be used for questions dealing with the structure of the organization, whilst FAQs (frequently asked questions) can be scripted to provide answers to the most likely queries. This in turn eliminates the need for a help line which, in the case of large multinational organizations with employees completing the survey in different time zones, would otherwise have to be staffed 24 hours a day.

Progress reporting and reminders

With an online study it is very straightforward to identify how well the study is progressing in terms of response rates. In turn, this means that it is possible to send out general reminders if the response to date is disappointing, or to dispense with any planned reminders if the response is above expectations. Where personal invitations to participate in the survey have been issued there is the possibility of targeting reminders, although it may damage the notion that the survey is anonymous.

Interim analyses can readily be performed with an online survey, and the full results can be available very soon after the deadline for completion has passed. One of the prime reasons for this immediacy is that the questionnaires do not have to be processed in the traditional sense, as this is done automatically given the right software. In turn this eliminates some of the cost attached to conducting a survey. However, it only represents one facet of the study, so it would be wrong to expect vast reductions in the price of a survey purely because it was moving from paper to online. There is also the danger of wasting time and effort in continually looking at the data throughout the fieldwork period simply because it is possible.

One worthwhile piece of analysis that can be performed, which is not possible with a paper questionnaire, is how long it typically takes for employees to complete the exercise. While an indication of how long it should take should be available from the planning stage and possibly a pilot study, it may well be that certain groups find it more difficult than others. This represents a learning that can be taken forward to future studies.

Distribution of results

In the same way that the processing of online questionnaires facilitates the reporting of progress during the survey period, it also helps when the time comes to report the results to all parts of the organization. The elimination of paper outputs means that it is much easier to provide data direct to those who are interested, say by division or country, and to do so in a timely fashion.

That the data is available on a central server also opens up the possibility of the database being interrogated for ad hoc analyses. With such possibilities come responsibilities, since it would clearly be wrong for unauthorized people to have access to any data, or to be able to analyse the data at a level that threatened the confidentiality of individual responses.

Multinational studies

There are many organizations with employees in different countries, which require questionnaires to be translated and subsequently aggregated to show a global picture. A web-based approach can help minimize the difficulties that sometimes arise with paper questionnaires at the translation stage, and also the overlay of results. In part this is a function of the control that can be exercised centrally when conducting studies of this type. These advantages are over and above those logistical ones that arise by virtue of not having to ship large amounts of paper around the world, at either the distribution or collation stages.

Verbatim comments

Increasingly as the proportion of employees who are comfortable using a PC grows, it would appear that responses to open questions are fuller than is the case with a paper questionnaire requiring handwritten responses. With the further benefit that there are no difficulties in reading typed responses, this is a particular area of strength for online surveys over a paper-based approach.

ISSUES FOR CONSIDERATION

Now we have considered the many benefits of online surveys, before automatically assuming that it is the approach to be adopted in all circumstances it is worth reflecting on some crucial issues that still have to be borne in mind.

Communication/timescales

The increased expectation of speed in turnaround of a survey can lead to a foreshortening of the timescales for the entire project, when the survey completion period is in fact only a part of a larger communication and engagement process. It therefore necessitates careful planning and a programme of communication that builds up to the survey itself.

Subsequently, and as a realization of any commitments offered in advance, there needs to be full reporting and involvement in action planning to determine what changes need to be implemented across the organization as a consequence of the survey.

Access to/distribution of questionnaires

A further danger arising from the above is that there can be pressure to limit the period during which employees are given the opportunity to complete the questionnaire. This can sometimes mean that the availability of people is overlooked: adequate time needs to be allowed for people being on holiday, training courses and other absences which could lead to them being 'disenfranchised' by virtue of the survey period being limited to the time they are away from the office.

Those who spend their days slaving over a PC also find it easy to assume that everyone has access to e-mail and the internet (and, indeed, that all those who do have a preference for completing a questionnaire at a PC as opposed to on paper). Yet there are large numbers of people, such as those working in customer-facing roles in shops or bank branches, who do not have such access. Even if they do, they may not be able to enter information about themselves in a manner that affords them the privacy they require or deserve.

With more and more people having access to a PC at home, it could be suggested that access in the office is not necessary. However it is important to give employees the choice whether they spend 'their' time completing a survey. In addition, the organization may wish to demonstrate the importance of the exercise by allowing people to complete it in company time.

One further provision that may have to be made concerns disabled employees. It has always been appropriate to consider the use of interviewers to administer questionnaires to such employees. With the progression to online surveys it is no less relevant to consider the involvement of interviewers or others who can assist them to complete a questionnaire. Indeed, with the advent of legislation such as the 1995 Disability Discrimination Act in the UK, the need to cater for disabled respondents so they are not precluded from taking part has potential legal force.

Confidentiality/independence

In addition to the point about privacy above, perceptions of confidentiality also arise with the hosting of the survey. Hosting on the website of a third party provides a similar reassurance to that obtained by providing reply-paid envelopes addressed to an external processor when paper questionnaires are used. For many people there can be a perceived risk of others (including their superiors) finding out their views if the information is collated internally.

This is also relevant to the use of passwords, which confer some benefits in managing an online survey, but which can add to the perception that an individual's responses will not remain anonymous. It is possible therefore, particularly when an online study is being conducted for the first time, that extra attention will need to be paid to reassuring those who might have these concerns.

Ultimately this all comes back to doing what most market researchers would do in the normal course of events, and that is thinking of the most appropriate approach given the business needs and the nature of the information required, rather than starting with a methodology and working back from that.

Proofreading and checking

Although web-based surveys have advantages of flexibility and immediacy, such benefits can introduce their own burden of care. Quite simply, what you see is not always what you want on screen. With a paper questionnaire, it is possible to check it quite readily for errors, especially if any routing is involved. Yet online such checking entails going through the permutations and combinations to ensure that all routes are correct and take respondents to the expected destination.

The very fact that changes can be made readily, and even late on in the process, sometimes means that time is not allowed for the more exhaustive level of checking required, with the potential consequence of wasted effort on the part of many respondents. It is therefore even more important that online surveys are piloted to identify any errors or flaws on the questionnaire.

Passwords and personal invitations

Mention has already been made of the use of passwords and personal invitations to participate in a survey, as opposed to a blanket request for participation. Without some mechanism for controlling the participation of individuals, typically involving a unique user ID and password, there is the danger of one person completing several questionnaires.

Personal invitations also offer real benefits to the employees themselves, since they allow them to interrupt the process of completing their questionnaire and return some time later to the point at which they broke off. Without this means of identifying their incomplete responses they would be required to start the process all over again. Also, if an incentive is being offered, say a prize draw, it is necessary to find a means of identifying those who took part.

However, as has also been noted such arrangements can give rise to concerns about the anonymity of a person's views, even though by the time the data is examined the link with an individual may not be evident. Where this is likely to be an issue it is possible to provide for individuals to choose their own passwords, which by definition are not known to anyone else.

Security and back-up

It is essential for any organization to implement sound arrangements to ensure the security and availability of data held on a computer system. The same principles apply to surveys in which employees are asked to give their views and opinions. Without adequate arrangements the data can only be restored by repeating the exercise, with a probable loss of confidence from the workforce. Equally, with large numbers of employees likely to be completing the questionnaires over an extended period, it is possible that more frequent back-up arrangements than normal will need to be made to avoid the loss of data since the previous back-up.

MRS INTERNET RESEARCH GUIDELINES

The MRS guidelines are concerned with the more generally applicable obligations placed upon researchers as they relate to the gathering of responses online. They also go into detail on some specific issues, such as those raised by research amongst children, which are not immediately relevant to this book. The following extracts highlight the more general principles behind conducting internet research.

Cooperation is voluntary

Researchers must avoid intruding unnecessarily on the privacy of internet respondents. Personal information (other than that already available from other sources) must not be sought from, or about, respondents without their prior knowledge and agreement. In addition, researchers must conform to any reasonable requests from respondents to delete data collected via internet surveys.

Respondents must not be inconvenienced

Where visitors to a particular website are asked to take part in a survey, either by clicking through to a survey site or via a pop-up window, care should be taken to ensure that those who do not wish to take part can easily exit or delete the survey. Respondents who have refused or completed a questionnaire must not be re-presented with the same survey for completion.

For internet surveys the likely length of the interview and thus the likely time commitment from respondents must be explained clearly. Respondents must not be deliberately misled regarding the likely time commitment. For non-pop-up internet surveys it should be made clear that respondents can complete the research at a time convenient to them, within the schedule dictated by the timeframe of the study.

Respondents should be given the opportunity to give a considered response (for example, to amend responses where necessary) and use 'don't know' or 'not applicable' responses where appropriate. At the end of the questionnaire or project, researchers should provide a thank-you statement or send an electronic thank-you letter, unless respondents have refused e-mail contact.

Respondents must give their informed consent

A description of the nature of the research must include the purpose of the survey (that is, market research), or, if the survey contains several topics, the broad variety of subject areas included in the questionnaire.

All the above information must be given at the start of the questionnaire, as should any links to data protection or privacy policies. This will ensure that should respondents fail to complete the questionnaire for any reason, their rights are protected.

In obtaining consent, researchers must not mislead the respondent about the nature of the research or the uses that will be made of the findings. It is however recognized that there are occasions on which, in order to prevent biased responses, the purpose of the research cannot be disclosed fully to respondents at the beginning of the interview. The researcher must avoid deceptive statements (which would be harmful or create a nuisance to the respondent), for example about the likely length of the interview or about the possibilities of being re-interviewed on a later occasion.

The researcher's identity must be disclosed

Respondents must be told the identity of the researcher/organization conducting the research and/or the client carrying out the project, along with a contact name and e-mail address at which they can be contacted. This could include a hyperlink to the researcher's home page for more information.

The respondent's anonymity must be safeguarded

The anonymity of respondents must be preserved unless they have given their informed consent for their details to be revealed. If respondents have given consent for data to be passed on in a form which allows them to be personally identified, the researcher must ensure that the information will only be used for the purposes that it was collected (that is, market research). Researchers can give this assurance via terms and conditions, contracts and so on. No such personally identifiable information may be used for subsequent purposes without the informed consent of the respondents. If consent is not given, the respondent should be reassured that confidentiality will be strictly maintained.

A respondent's e-mail address is personal data and must therefore be treated as such within the purpose of MRS Code of Conduct and data protection legislation.

Safeguarding data

Researchers must post a privacy policy statement on their online site (including any restricted access survey sites). The policy statements should be easy to find, easy to use and clearly written. Typically a statement sets out how any information gathered in a visit to the site will be used, and whether this includes the use of 'cookies'.

Researchers must offer respondents adequate security in the transmission of sensitive data. Researchers must also ensure that any confidential information provided to them by clients or others is protected (for example by a firewall or encryption) against unauthorized access.

Before personal data is sent over the internet to another country, researchers must check with the relevant authority (such as a data protection regulator) that the data transfer is permissible. The recipient may need to provide safeguards necessary for the protection of the data, since certain countries do not have equivalent data protection legislation.

Researchers must adequately protect personal data collected or stored on websites or servers. Especially sensitive or valuable information should be protected by reliable encryption techniques.

If temporary storage of the personal data collected takes place on a server that is operated by a third-party provider, the research agency must place the provider under the obligation to take the necessary precautions to ensure that third parties cannot access the data on the server or during data transfer. Temporary storage of the collected data on the server must be terminated at the earliest possible time.

Researchers must have adequate safeguards in place to ensure that when e-mails are sent in batches the e-mail addresses of the respondents are not revealed to other respondents. Clients must be fully informed about the potential risk of posting details of confidential organization information in internet questionnaires.

CONCLUSIONS

Employee surveys, especially those designed to engage whole organizations in dialogue, have historically tended to be based on paper questionnaires completed by the employees themselves. Such a methodology has lent itself very readily to a web-based approach.

The principal advantages of web-based questionnaires are by now fairly obvious and well known. Not only does the technology permit more flexibility and assist with a more rapid turnaround, it is also far easier to keep track of how the survey is going during the fieldwork period. In conjunction with the use of e-mail to communicate with employees (before, during and after the survey) online surveys represent a very efficient and effective way of conducting such surveys.

However, it is essential that the requirements of any study dictate the methodology used and not the other way around. Moreover, the fundamental principles of conducting an employee survey still have to be adhered to, while attention is paid to the implications that stem from the use of the very technology that is bringing the benefits outlined.

7 Qualitative research

INTRODUCTION

Although arguably it forms a more youthful branch of research, qualitative techniques have matured to the point that there is now general acceptance of their validity and the benefits of their use. In particular, whereas quantitative research offers measurement, qualitative research is better equipped to provide explanations and understanding of why people do things, or the reasons for holding the beliefs and attitudes that they do.

This chapter therefore considers what qualitative research is and how it differs from quantitative research. Specifically it looks at the skill set required of a qualitative researcher, before going on to examine some of the issues specific to, and applications of, qualitative research amongst employees.

The applications of qualitative research are considered under three main headings: when it is undertaken prior to a quantitative study, following a quantitative study, and independently of any quantification. In addition, those qualitative applications are considered that involve both employees and customers in the research, as well as any solely concerned with employees.

SPECIFIC FEATURES OF QUALITATIVE RESEARCH

Whereas quantitative research is steeped in such disciplines as statistical theory, qualitative research has its roots in the sciences of psychology and anthropology. It involves an approach that is more flexible than the structured questionnaire that underpins any quantification. Qualitative research is therefore concerned with exploring motivations and understanding attitudes, and how those attitudes influence behaviour. Through its inherent flexibility it also offers a medium that can foster creativity and be used to stimulate and develop ideas and concepts.

Another substantial point of difference between the two broad forms of research is that quantitative research usually seeks to represent the views of the universe or population under study. In the extreme this can involve conducting a census: that is, seeking to gather the views of everyone. Indeed, as explained in a previous chapter this approach is much more common in employee research than other categories of research because of the importance of being seen to involve everybody in an organization and to give them all the opportunity to have their say. With most organizations the size of the workforce is such that it is a practical proposition to involve everyone, unlike other populations in research.

By contrast, because qualitative research is more about gaining an understanding and explanation of issues, rather than the measurement of something, it is more important to talk to enough people to obtain a spread of views, in the knowledge that there will be diminishing returns in the opinions that can be put forward by speaking to additional people. Sometimes this is referred to as theoretical sampling saturation.

Essentially, the tenth person spoken to is not likely to add as many new points as it would have been open for the first, second or third person to add. It is therefore feasible to identify a consensus of core views by speaking to a relatively small number of people. What is important in an employee context is to represent the spread of views that may exist, say, from different functional areas, different regions, or different grades and levels (managerial, supervisory, clerical and so on).

The toolkit available to the qualitative researcher includes techniques that involve observation of respondents' behaviour, although the predominant forms are the group discussion (sometimes referred to as a focus group) and the in-depth interview. Group discussions are typically formed by a moderator and six to eight respondents, which is the optimal size to ensure that each respondent can contribute, while at the same time not unduly extending the time taken up by the discussion (typically between one and two hours).

One of the hallmarks of running a group discussion is the ability to benefit from the dynamics that operate within the group. As with any group of people the interactions between the individuals that comprise it can be positive or negative. The aim of the moderator is therefore to minimize any possible disruption or adverse effects while maximizing the positive interactions which allow individuals to build on the ideas and thought processes of others in the group. Indeed, during the course of the discussions individuals may come to reappraise their own thoughts and contribution in the light of comments made by others.

The size of a group discussion is variable, and the phrase 'mini-group' has been coined to denote those with a smaller number of participants, say four or five. Meanwhile, larger and longer gatherings are likely to be styled as 'extended' groups or even workshops, where the intent is still the same: to engage a group of people, to ascertain their views and to develop thinking in a given area. The fundamental requirement, as embodied in the Market Research Society Code of Conduct, is that those agreeing to take part do so in full knowledge of what is expected of them and what will happen to the results from the research.

Following on from the point above about representing the spread of opinions, in the group context it is crucial not to mix participants in such a way that some may be inhibited by the presence of others. Although in consumer research it does occasionally happen that 'conflict groups' are purposely conducted to pit those with contrasting, even opposing, views against each other, such approaches clearly have to be handled extremely carefully. In employee research there are other considerations that must be observed, not least because, unlike those who gather on a single evening for a consumer group discussion, employees could be in frequent contact with other participants following an employee group. Moreover, the most likely reason for inhibition is the presence of someone in authority over an individual (his or her manager or supervisor). Consequently employee group discussions tend to be made up of those from comparable levels across the organization.

As with group discussions, where there is not an absolute for the number of participants, in-depth interviews do not always consist of a single respondent. The notions of paired or even triangular interviews were developed largely to accommodate the juxtaposition of different perspectives. In consumer research paired interviews may be used to explore decision making in a household by talking to, say, a married couple. In business, and among employees of a company, they could be used to bring together parties involved in different stages of a process with a view to identifying ways in which that process could be improved. There is the additional benefit of being able to cover more ground, on the basis that two people jointly would have a wider perspective than one.

Aside from such possibilities, depth interviews tend to be conducted on a one-to-one basis, and this highlights the contrast between interviews conducted for the purposes of qualitative research and those completed as part of a quantitative study. Whereas a quantitative interview will follow a very structured questionnaire, qualitative research relies on a discussion (or topic) guide. This guide in effect constitutes an agenda for the discussion or interview, which will have been agreed by the researcher and the person commissioning the research in advance. Yet it is critical that the structure is flexible to accommodate the flow of thoughts from the respondent. While the intention will always be to cover the entire agenda by the end of the interview, the order in which the topics are dealt with, and the weight given to any one, have to reflect the relative importance to the interviewee, rather than the presumption of the moderator or the end-user of the research findings.

Irrespective of which technique is used, it is important to conduct sufficient interviews and/or groups for the understanding gained from them to grow and develop. The fact that the respondents themselves are influencing the agenda for the research means that the first interview or group will rarely be handled in an identical fashion to the last one. Some hypotheses that may have been present in the initial phase of a project will have been rejected, while fresh ones will have been explored and developed. Moreover, this iterative aspect of qualitative research facilitates (and almost demands) a parallel iterative approach between the researcher and the commissioner of the research through a series of regular updates. Failure to do so will mean that the client is unaware of, and unable to contribute to, the development of the thinking during the course of the project.

THE SKILLS REQUIRED OF A QUALITATIVE RESEARCHER

The above requirements dictate the need for the researcher moderating the discussion to be skilled in several ways. On the surface, running a group discussion can appear to be no more arduous than chatting to a few acquaintances. However, for the research to be productive and achieve its aims the moderator needs to be able to do all of the things set out below.

The moderator must be able to readily involve and engage respondents. One and a half hours is not long to extract the views and opinions of seven or eight people, so they need to be engaged rapidly. Those who are familiar with Tuckman's (1965) description of the development of teams will appreciate that the stages of 'forming, storming, norming and performing' need to be executed with speed within such a timescale. The moderator therefore needs to be able to make respondents feel at ease quickly and ensure that they contribute to the discussion.

Having engaged the participants, the moderator must chair the discussion without imposing any personal views. Although moderators are 'in charge' there is little point if they act as though chairing a meeting and proceed to communicate their own views at length when the main purpose is to find out what the respondents think. Clearly anyone moderating will have their own views and prejudices, but these have to be left at the door when they enter the room to perform their role.

The chairing of the discussion demands that the views of all participants are elicited whilst it is crucial that no individuals are allowed to dominate the discussion. Intriguingly, in much employee research the efforts of the moderator may also have to be deployed in curtailing the discussion at the end of the session, often to the dismay of those who may have doubted in advance that their employees would open up at all. In these situations it is possibly a reflection on the limited opportunities that employees otherwise have to air their views on life in the organization.

The operation of this safety valve, allowing employees to 'let off steam', can be critical to the process of engaging them in the discussion even if the subject matter is far removed from the agenda for it. The outputs can also be reported back to the client as part of the broader understanding to be gained from the project, although it is important to manage the amount of time taken by this element of the discussion prior to moving on to the main agenda for the research.

As well as not coming with preconceived notions or prejudices, it is important that the moderator is seen as independent, both in giving participants freedom to speak up (something they may not do as readily if the moderator is known to them) and in the interpretation of their views. Typically therefore those undertaking qualitative research will be drawn from outside the organization. This being the case it is critical that any moderators are briefed fully on the organization without in any way biasing their perspective. They need to understand the politics and the tensions that may exist between different areas of the organization so that they can allow for them and even deal with them if they are in danger of disrupting or distorting the discussion.

While the ability to analyse and interpret what is said is clearly a major requirement, it is equally important to take account of what is not said. Whether it is in the form of non-verbal signals (posture, gestures and so on) or simply what is left unsaid by respondents, the moderator needs to be able to gather all such inputs, as well as what is actually spoken, and analyse the totality of the responses. Although he was not specifically talking about research, a very relevant quotation comes again from Peter Drucker, who said 'The most important thing in communication is to hear what isn't being said.'

Lines of enquiry have to be developed, modified and closed off as the conversation unfolds. The analytical abilities required are therefore both 'active' (in the sense of controlling the flow of the discussion as it happens) and 'reflective' (making sense of the aggregated responses of all participants at the end of the research). The premium placed on good analytical skills and judgement at the completion of the research is reinforced by the fact that it has to be undertaken, by definition, without the support of hard, statistical evidence.

In many respects moderators are themselves role-playing, ranging from acting as spokespersons who represent various points of view to being chameleon-like, adapting their interventions to the flow of the discussion. This may seem at odds with the need for objectivity (almost to the point of transparency) but particularly where the discussion is being used to stimulate ideas and develop concepts, it can require the moderator to put forward ideas (through the use of stimulus material such as concept boards and other projective techniques) that the participants need to build on. It therefore becomes part of the engagement activity, as the concepts are quite likely to be ones that the participants would have had no reason to think about before attending the discussion.

At the conclusion of a qualitative stage of research, a moderator similarly has to display the dual skills of independence and advocacy. When reporting or presenting findings from the research, it is essential that he or she is seen to be neutral and objective in his/her assessment yet capable of being persuasive in recommending courses of action based on the research undertaken. The greatest danger in any such exercise is that the information gathered during the research process is not used and acted upon. The moderator therefore has a primary role in identifying the most appropriate courses of action and then persuading those who commissioned the research to see those actions through.

ISSUES SPECIFIC TO QUALITATIVE RESEARCH AMONGST EMPLOYEES

It has already been noted above that there are considerations that have to be borne in mind when conducting qualitative research amongst employees, over and above those that might be observed in the conduct of consumer research. Hence the need to consider the composition of respondents in a group discussion so as to avoid, say, any inhibitions arising from the presence of people from different levels in the organization's hierarchy.

Confidentiality and anonymity

Concerns about the confidentiality of any opinions expressed have to be recognized and dealt with. Employees, even if they are not shareholders in an organization, can have substantial personal investment in it. Indeed, setting aside other monetary benefits linked to the organization (such as pensions, bonuses, loans for property or vehicles) the cumulative value of a career, including the potential for further advancement, could be perceived as being in jeopardy if they are deemed to express views which are not acceptable to others.

Someone who is attending a focus group as a customer of an organization is risking little in expressing a critical opinion of that organization. Indeed, one of the virtues of market research is that it helps organizations identify where they need to make corrections and improve what they offer to existing and potential customers. By contrast, as can be seen by the treatment of more publicized 'whistleblowers', organizations can easily take against 'one of their own' who has the courage to point out shortcomings in their practices. A National Whistleblower Center survey (as reported on their website) of 200 random whistleblower reports made to the Washington, DC-based watchdog group during 2002 found 49.5 per cent reported that they were fired for blowing the whistle. And these were not trivial cases since over half of these respondents said they had reported fraud or criminal practices.

It is therefore critical that employees are reassured of the confidentiality of anything they may say in a focus group or depth interview. This of course is particularly relevant when, as is common, a moderator or interviewer wishes to record groups (on tape or disk) for the purposes of analysis later. Few researchers are blessed with perfect recall, so the use of recordings permits an exhaustive analysis, ensuring that all views are accorded due weight.

That said, it is imperative that permission to record is requested in advance of the interview or discussion taking place, and if an employee declines then it will be necessary for the moderator to make notes of the discussion or have a note-taker present. Whilst this is less satisfactory from the researcher's point of view, that should not be allowed to compromise the integrity and confidentiality of the research process.

This in turn makes it highly unlikely that employee groups will be recorded on visual rather than audio media, as is often the case in consumer research. The use of video in consumer research is a powerful means of demonstrating to decision makers how customers feel about an issue, and it is extremely unlikely that any one respondent would be known to those executives being shown the video. In contrast, any employee recorded on video would be readily identifiable and any guarantees of anonymity that they may have received would quickly be rendered worthless. For the same reason the practice of allowing observers to attend consumer groups cannot be replicated within an employee study.

Coverage of the research

The composition of a group discussion may also have implications for the way in which certain topics are covered in the research. When individuals from, say, different backgrounds, with varying political (both internal and party-political) allegiances, are brought together it is possible that some discussions (for example, relating to equal opportunities) could get heated, again with the dangers of greater 'fall-out' than is ever likely from a similar sized gathering of respondents drawn from the general public. The key here lies not in the avoidance of such issues but in the anticipation of those that might excite. The necessary preparations can then be made, not least with the use of a skilled moderator.

Sensitivity over the topics to be discussed may also be pertinent in organizations where large numbers of the workforce are represented by trade unions. It represents good practice where unions are involved to inform them of plans for any research and to gain their commitment to the process. Apart from anything else this makes it possible to allay any misconceptions that could otherwise arise over whether the discussions might cut across more formal negotiations. In some respects the flexibility and free-flowing nature of any group discussions (as opposed to the certainty of a structured questionnaire) make it as important to engage unions in the qualitative research process as it is with a quantitative study.

A time and a place

Since group discussions can easily last for an hour and a half, and interviews take up to an hour, it is important to consider whether they are scheduled to take place during or outside the working day. While it is standard practice for consumer groups to take place during the evening, this reflects the fact that few people would be able or prepared to take time off work to participate in such research. With employees, the situation is virtually reversed in that they are less likely to want to spent time of their own discussing work-related topics.

The point here is further complicated by the difficulties of thanking people for their participation in the same way as is traditional with consumer research: by means of a cash gift, vouchers or even goods such as a bottle of whisky. A practical dimension to this issue is that the tax authorities would regard these payments as taxable (as either pay or a benefit in kind). In addition, there is always a philosophical preference for having participants who are there by virtue of an interest in the subject matter rather than those who are attending as a means of increasing their income.

A solution that meets this need while avoiding the complications of involving payroll departments and tax authorities is to hold the research sessions over extended lunch breaks (and possibly outside work hours, provided the occasion is presented as an attractive event in its own right). It will be attractive if the subject matter under discussion is of interest, and potential respondents are made to feel they will be able to make a genuine contribution through their participation. It should also be enjoyable; the location is crucial to this and the provision of food and refreshments will also help.

If the research is conducted after the working day there are generally more possibilities for holding the sessions off-site. It has to be recognized that those with families or burdened with long working hours may be reluctant to become involved at this time. Where it can be arranged, participants are more likely to arrive free of some of the 'baggage' attached to their job and be more open-minded on some of the issues to be discussed. The optimal timing will vary according to the place of work. In large conurbations, such as London, employees will arrive at work from all points of the compass having commuted significant distances. In order to facilitate their return home it is suggested that the timing of any research activity follows closely on the end of the normal working day. Elsewhere in the country, it may be appropriate to schedule the event for later to allow employees, should they wish, to go home prior to reconvening at a central point for the research.

The benefits of the above approach apply particularly to group discussions, involving as they do a number of participants. The reasons for conducting interviews off-site are less compelling. Indeed, it is often the case that more senior people are interviewed alone, and the demands on their time are such that it makes practical sense to talk to them in their offices. There will occasionally be compelling logistical reasons for holding group discussions in the workplace. Even so attention needs to be given to the location of the discussions. For instance, there may be nervousness on the part of some employees if the group is held in a meeting room that is located in an area where their participation would be noted by other, possibly more senior colleagues.

Reporting back

The need to feed back the results, plus accompanying actions, arising from any employee research is a message that bears repetition. Nowhere is the message more important than in qualitative research. By definition a small proportion of the workforce will have participated at length in an exercise where they have been invited to contribute to the debate on issues of significance to the organization.

The participation alone can be a very powerful form of motivation, as the individuals concerned will derive a strong sense of involvement in the decision-making process. However, this can easily backfire if the participants are left without any indication as to what will happen following the research. The perceived return on their investment of time and effort will quickly become a loss if they are not informed how matters will be taken forward. Even a decision to take a contrary course of action to that recommended in the research can be accepted if it is accompanied by a rationale. Complete silence on any decision making is likely to result in reluctance on the part of those respondents to participate in future activities.

It is recognized that in certain instances the nature of the subject matter and the implications of the decisions will be such that all employees (and possibly external audiences) should be advised simultaneously. Even so, it should be possible to explain this to those who took part, and their contribution should certainly be recognized when the announcement is finally made. Apart from demonstrating an appreciation of these contributions, this can also create a positive impression among the workforce generally.

The fact that employees will have taken part in the research on the basis that their identities are not revealed to the employer inevitably requires that their contributions are recognized in a general way, such as through a communication to all employees. A more direct and targeted thank-you message can only be delivered by the external moderator, who can arrange for a personalized communication without the recipients ever being identified by those working for the organization.

APPLICATIONS OF QUALITATIVE RESEARCH

Although there are clear differences, as outlined previously, between qualitative and quantitative research, the two are frequently used in tandem, providing the organization with the benefits that each can bring to decision making. This section therefore sets out the combination of ways in which they can be used and the benefits of so doing.

Prior to a quantitative study

One of the great dangers of constructing a questionnaire for a quantitative study is to do so without any input from those who will be asked to complete it. Quite simply if the questions are irrelevant to, and do not address the issues of, respondents they will not want to complete it. It will have failed to offer them any benefits or rationale for completion. To compound matters, there is the danger that the message communicated by the organization to its employees will effectively be that their views are not important and that the organization is only collecting data it regards as important.

Examples of where this can occur in employee research are when the focus of those commissioning the research is solely on the measurement of progress against some organizational objectives or some external benchmarks. This is not to say that such measurement should not be undertaken, rather that a balance needs to be struck. The opportunity for employees to express their own views about working in the organization needs to be given comparable weight to the information gathered from employees for the benefit of the organization. Ironically, the harmony evident in a balanced questionnaire that serves both purposes well is likely to be found in an organization that has previously invested considerable time and effort in gathering the views of employees. The imperative to conduct a preliminary stage of qualitative research is therefore likely to be greatest in organizations without the culture or history of collating inputs from employees.

More specifically qualitative research can play a number of roles in advance of a quantitative project. It can be a means of gathering ideas and issues, and of determining what is important to employees. The flexibility and scope for creativity within qualitative disciplines is crucial here. By contrast, a quantitative questionnaire works well when it is offering respondents predetermined lists of issues or attributes to choose from or to rank; it is less effective at gathering responses that are over and above those specifically requested.

The typical way in which the latter might be attempted in a quantitative exercise, through the use of an open question in a self-completion questionnaire (without the involvement of an interviewer), inevitably means that it lacks the prompting or stimulation that many people require. In addition, the motivation to spend additional time thinking about the issues involved may be lacking when respondents have been informed that the questionnaire will only take a few minutes of their time and they have other things to get on with.

By contrast, involvement in a qualitative interview or group discussion will have been set up as taking a given amount of time. Moreover, inherently, the presence of an interviewer or moderator can act as the catalyst for generating ideas and trawling below the superficial responses that might be given without further prompting. It can therefore generate a wealth of suggestions for the issues that are important to employees, as well as being used as a preliminary filter in those situations where it is necessary to allocate some order of priority.

In addition to using qualitative research to set the 'agenda' of any questionnaire, another major role is in refining it. Prior knowledge and/ or organizational requirements may have resulted in an agenda that is already established. Here, in addition to assessing how well this compares with an agenda that employees would create themselves, it is important to check whether the way in which questions are posed is appropriate to that organization.

While there are dangers in taking questions created elsewhere and modifying them (if the intention is to benchmark against other organizations, a variation in the wording may invalidate the comparison) there is equally the danger of using language that is alien to the employees of an organization. Every organization has its own culture and language (notably the use of acronyms and abbreviations) so the way in which questions are phrased can be off-putting to potential respondents if it is not in keeping with how such matters are normally expressed internally. At worst, of course, the questions could be deemed as being irrelevant to employees if they do not relate to their experience or perception of what is important in their own organization.

Qualitative research is here being asked to play a role in piloting, as discussed in Chapter 5. Apart from any other consideration, it is worth remembering that a pilot study can be a particularly good investment. All too often it is seen as time-consuming when those commissioning a major study have their own views as to what should be covered in it. Yet as can be seen from the Cadbury's case study, a pilot study can end up with a strong rationale for saving the expenditure that would have been incurred if the full study went ahead.

Following a quantitative study

Classically, quantitative research is used for measurement, with various statistical techniques being deployed to examine causal relationships between variables identified in the study. However, without the ability to forecast the results of any survey it is not possible to include all those factors that might have contributed to any result. Consequently, it is not always the case that a full explanation can be interpreted from the data alone.

Happily, qualitative research is particularly useful in determining the root causes of behaviours and attitudes. For instance, a quantitative survey may have identified that there are low levels of satisfaction and that stress levels are high. Following this up with a qualitative exploration of stress and the specific causes should make it possible to ascertain the underlying problems and to identify possible solutions.

In addition, it may well be that attitudes and behaviours vary between different types of employee. For instance, managers and non-managerial employees may well have different expectations of and attitudes towards the organization they work for, by virtue of their length of association with, personal investment in or emotional attachment to that organization. By exploring the relevant issues with managers and non-managerial employees in separate qualitative sessions, the differences of opinion can be determined and if appropriate acted upon.

This in turn highlights another major way in which qualitative techniques may be used following a quantitative survey: to support action plans and target setting. Once the issues arising from a survey and the reasons behind them have been identified, the next stage is to plan so that all of the issues requiring attention are dealt with. Since these issues have been identified with the input of the workforce, it makes eminent sense to continue that input through to its conclusion and issue resolution.

Again, the nature of group discussions or workshops, involving larger numbers of employees, is very well suited to generating ideas and solutions. The labels of workshops and group discussions may appear to be used interchangeably, and in many respects they both are broadly concerned with gathering inputs from employees with a view to implementing change. Without being overly concerned with definitions, it is worth reflecting on the distinctions between the two approaches so as not to perpetuate any confusion.

Workshops are more likely to be composed of people who are there because of the position in the organization, and therefore the viewpoint or perspective that they represent. Indeed, it is possible that a workshop will transcend different hierarchical levels, since the agenda is to find solutions rather than express more personal views. The person charged with leading the workshop, although still likely to be independent (and hence impartial) of all participants, will act as a facilitator, ensuring that the inputs from different levels and areas are considered and weighed before conclusions are finally reached. If it acts in this way, the organization is more likely to obtain the support of all groups as it moves forward, instead of imposing solutions that are not supported.

Consequently the parties attending the workshop are quite likely to go away with specific responsibilities for actions that have been agreed. While this may also happen following a group discussion, the tasks given to such respondents are more likely to be a continuation of the process of gathering knowledge rather than the implementation of decisions.

In essence, qualitative research in the form of group discussions is used to provide an understanding of the attitudes and motivations of employees, along with such things as the language that is employed within the organization. Workshops are more likely to be concerned with helping the organization move forward in the light of the information gathered from the research.

Independent of quantification

It is sometimes the case (notably where a workforce is very small) that research amongst employees is done exclusively on a qualitative basis, without any accompanying quantitative research. However, the main reason that so much qualitative research is conducted amongst employees relates to the issues researched. In the same way that customer research is conducted across a wide spectrum of topics (from communications, products and services, to packaging and design, and so on), when employees are the recipients of a communication, or benefit from the facilities afforded to them by the organization, there is a role for qualitative research in the development of these messages and services.

In addition, and as foreshadowed in Chapter 2, where employees are an integral part of service delivery to the customers of an organization, it makes it eminently sensible to gather the views of both groups in any research undertaken. This section therefore considers areas in which qualitative research is undertaken among both groups, before examining those situations where employees are the primary audience in any research.

Qualitative research among both customers and employees

The spectrum of situations here ranges from those where employees are genuinely customers of the organization in their own right, through to those where they are 'bystanders', who could be affected by overhearing communications that are aimed at customers, but reflect on them and may unwittingly impact on their self-regard.

Where employees are genuinely purchasers of an organization's goods and services they can have additional and beneficial insights and suggestions for the development of new offerings, or the refinement of existing ones. Since research of this type is largely a process of creative development, it is usually undertaken through the medium of qualitative research in order to maximize the constructive dynamics of running group discussions. Not only does the forum encourage the sparking of ideas between participants, it can also facilitate the evaluation of those ideas. This can work at both the strategic level (perhaps looking at which markets the organization has the potential to operate in) and the tactical level (developing and refining the detail of what is offered in a given market), although there are dangers in attempting to do both in the same piece of research, as neither would be explored in sufficient depth.

More commonly, research among employees will be conducted as part of customer research projects because they are an integral part of the interaction between customers and the employing organization. Most service industries, by definition, deliver their offerings through employees, and as a result the employees need to be 'sold' the service so they can in turn sell it to the end customer. Although the development of a new service might be to the satisfaction of customers, if there is an aspect of it that is unattractive to employees the result could be a loss of business to the organization. Such difficulties could easily arise from the way employees are remunerated, with the consequence that they devote more time to the sales of services that offer higher incentives. If the new service does not fit the incentive scheme, this could affect its sales performance. Simply conducting research among customers (to whom the concept of the service is very appealing) would not reveal the actual cause of the low volume of sales.

To turn to overhearing, the typical situation in which this arises is in the use of above-the-line or mass-media advertising, such as campaigns that feature employees in advertising aimed primarily at customers. Since the development cycle for these campaigns is likely to involve the use of qualitative research amongst existing and potential customers (for the strategic development of the overall campaign as well as at the executional level of individual advertisements) it represents very little in terms of additional expense to conduct some separate research at each stage among employees. It would be ironic not to do this, for example if employees are meant to be portrayed as the heroes of the campaign but no one bothers to ask any employees whether they regard themselves as such.

For another example, take the retail sector and the large investments made in the design of outlets. Clearly the design has to be attractive to consumers, but it is also worth sparing a thought for those who have to work in that environment all day and every day. When banks belatedly recognized that their branches were indeed retail outlets, there was a rush to alter the layout and ambience of many branches, introducing such things as coffee bars and piped music. One December a bank decided to play a limited selection of carols continuously. The customer response was very appreciative, but many staff soon sought to turn the music off, as listening to the same tape over and over again can be testing even for the most ardent devotee.

Qualitative research amongst employees as the primary audience

As with customers there is a wide range of communications media that can be deployed to communicate internally. So, in the same way that research features prominently in the development of customer communications, at both strategic and tactical levels, it makes sense to consider similar approaches to the development of internal communication. While the relationship between the expenditure on research and that on, say, an in-house publication (with spend registered in the thousands) is not as compelling as it might be with external advertising (where the spend can be registered in the millions), there are clearly risks associated with getting the communication wrong and alienating the workforce.

At the strategic level, employees could be convened in group discussions to consider the portfolio of communications media, to examine the relative effectiveness at achieving their aims and to explore areas in which information is considered to be lacking. More targeted research can then be used to assess the suitability of specific media to convey specific messages, and to give guidance on the best way of executing this. Here it is important to consider the breadth of any research, as there can be considerable discrepancies in the way in which different parts of the organization will respond to the same messages, and research can help identify how the communication should be tailored to take account of this.

Away from internal communications, employees can also be described as users of services provided by their employer in the form of benefits. The development of these services warrants the same sort of input from employees that customers make through product development research. A particular case in point is the offering by employers of a 'cafeteria' benefit plan, whereby employees can select from a range of benefit options. This requires an approach akin to market segmentation, as different groups of employees (defined by gender or age, for instance) are likely to opt for different combinations. It is therefore essential that preparatory work is done to identify the extent of the range required to meet the needs of the different groups.

For example Global Home Loans, the third-party mortgage administrator, decided to introduce a new benefits scheme in stages. Extensive group discussions were held to ensure it was something that staff wanted and appreciated. A different application of qualitative research comes from the UK regulatory authorities, where one such body was anticipating significant changes to its role (see below).

CASE STUDY

With the increasing priority given to pensions and associated issues, and the introduction of new pensions legislation, Opra (the Occupational Pensions Regulatory Authority) had to think about the best way of transforming itself into the Pensions Regulator – the more flexible, proactive, risk-focused authority that was required to meet the new challenges. To this end, the HR team was to be reorganized in order to drive through changes in the workplace and maintain staff commitment.

Opra commissioned KW Research, an experienced independent agency, to conduct a qualitative research project in order to evaluate how staff viewed the HR changes that were going on within the organization in preparation for the transition to the Pensions Regulator. Three group discussions, six paired and 17 in-depth interviews were convened by employee research specialists among a representative sample of management and staff, which included HR personnel; additionally, 26 other individuals responded to the opportunity to comment via confidential one-page questionnaires which were obtained from the intranet and, once completed, mailed direct to the research agency. Understandably, research at this time was likely to be characterized by some anxious and demotivated attitudes, with some strong views emerging from the self-selected, self-completion online respondents.

Recruitment to the in-depth sessions was carried out in Opra's Research Department, but the identity of participating respondents remained absolutely confidential to all directorates, including the HR department. Respondents' permission to tape record the sessions was gained at interview, and data thus obtained was subject to the rigorous controls of the Data Protection Act, in strict accordance with the Market Research Society's Code of Conduct and in keeping with Opra's union safeguards.

Research was required to explore reactions to the new HR approach, determine expectations from each function, assess the potential impact of the new approach, and establish future priorities for the HR team. The results were enlightening and extremely valuable. Despite the instability of their own positions, this intelligent and thoughtful workforce recognized the need for fundamental organizational change, driven by forthcoming legislation, to improve the service they offered to their clients – those working in the pensions industry. Internal information was perceived to be at a premium, however, and this fuelled anxieties and concerns at this key time. The new HR structure was conceptually appealing, but was seen to be at odds with the former philosophy of the department, so a seismic shift was needed to change the culture.

More importantly, it emerged that the HR function and department represented a microcosm of the organization itself: if the HR department could transform itself effectively to meet the standards required by the new Pensions Regulator, then so could the whole organization. Implementation and communication were major concerns, and thus it was essential to draw up a schedule of actions during the final stage of research, which included a brainstorming day involving all HR personnel run by Kate Willis.

To monitor reactions to the transformation, an ongoing quantitative assessment is to be scheduled annually.

QUALITATIVE RESEARCH ONLINE

The case study on Opra includes a simple example of how qualitative feedback can be supplemented by gathering views online. Chapter 6 outlined more broadly the various forms of research that together constitute online research. While there is little dispute about the opportunities opened up by the internet in the conduct of quantitative research, there is less unanimity on the efficacy of conducting qualitative research online.

At one level the existence of a chat room on the internet is a demonstration of a form of a discussion group. Chat rooms generally are not subject to the careful selection and recruitment of participants that typifies formal research. Frequently they will not be subject to any form of moderation either. However, it is clear that one can conduct an exchange of views between two or more people online.

What is lacking from such online exchanges is the ability to capture and interpret the non-verbal inputs that contribute so much to the meaning derived from traditional interviews and group discussions. In time the quality of video-conferencing links will assist, although there will still be debate whether the interactions between individuals onscreen will be as powerful as those when they are gathered in the same room.

Where online discussions do readily assist is by doing away with the need for transcribing. Traditional qualitative research has relied on transcripts of audio recordings to furnish the moderator with a complete record of what was said. Since online participants are expressing their views freely (and quite possibly more honestly than they would do in the physical presence of others) in text that is digitally captured, it means that the outputs can be transferred readily to sophisticated analytical tools designed to assist with the interpretation of the language used.

When the communication is simply in the form of text it is of course necessary to be aware that some things that are written are much easier to misconstrue than when they are spoken. Against this, there will be situations when it is advantageous to extend the discussion over a longer period than is normally possible, even to several days. This can facilitate new directions and interventions while retaining the involvement of a given group of people, something that is unlikely to be possible with a conventional group discussion.

CONCLUSIONS

By its very nature, qualitative research has the potential to be more flexible than quantitative research, and consequently treat matters in a holistic fashion that a more focused quantitative questionnaire cannot.

It can therefore be used in a manner that facilitates discovery and understanding, with the advantage of doing so in an iterative fashion as hypotheses are developed and tested.

Ultimately, qualitative research, conducted either in conjunction with a quantitative survey or on its own, has the capacity to inform decision making in a way that provides a rationale for action.

As with any other form of research there are fundamentals that need to be observed to ensure that the time and effort devoted to it are productive. Chief amongst these are the support and buy-in of senior management and the feedback of any results and actions arising from the research.

8 The advent of employee insight

INTRODUCTION

Previous chapters have highlighted the importance of considering employee research in the broader context of communications taking place in an organization. This chapter is essentially recognition of the need to integrate all of an organization's sources of data and information about employees, including that derived from employee research. As such it is a parallel development of the concept that has emerged in consumer marketing and research.

Among the marketing and market research fraternities the concept of customer insight represents the need and desire to extract more value and direction from information gathered, for the benefit of the business concerned. Interestingly, at the same time HR functions have become more integrated within and aligned to the management and business of their organizations.

In terms of remits, the market research and HR functions could be characterized as being concerned traditionally with the opinions of customers and employees respectively. Unfortunately, in too many instances this has meant that information about these two critical audiences has been gathered in isolation and not harnessed for the benefit of the organization.

This chapter therefore considers the different perspectives of these functions, and argues for the need to maximize the collection and usage of data so that the organization achieves the goal of being more insightful about the current and potential contributions of the people who work for it.

THE EVOLUTION OF A DISCIPLINE – MR

Although the Market Research Society in the UK has been running annual conferences for over half a century, it was not until the 1970s that papers about research among employees began to feature. Indeed, it was not until 1996 that an entire session, consisting of three papers, was devoted to the subject of employee research.

Schlackman, Thornley and Vuillamy (1970) described a study involving a relocation of offices, and the role research played in identifying the amenities employees hoped to have access to in their new surroundings. Then in 1973 Bob Worcester discussed the way in which employee research could be used to assist companies in raising the effectiveness of their dealings with external publics.

By the end of that decade, in his address to the 1979 ESOMAR Congress on Information for Management, Frank Teer was able to espouse the notion that the role of the information director was the logical successor to that of the market research manager. He noted how market research roles had broadened, taking in the employee and social dimensions over and above the traditional ones of supporting the marketing function. Yet he was still aware that more needed to be done to fully integrate the contribution of market research to the business in which it operated. In particular, this necessitated a more strategic approach, akin to how the finance director was contributing to decision making in ways in which a bookkeeper never could or would.

More than a quarter of a century on, research functions in many organizations have been remodelled as insight functions. As well as addressing a broader range of issues, this has involved adopting a more inclusive approach to information sources, notably that emanating from customer databases.

CUSTOMER INSIGHT

Stone, Bond and Foss, in *Consumer Insight* (2004), and Wills and Williams in 'Insight as a strategic asset' (also 2004), describe how insight is more than a relabelling of the market research or customer database functions. While some organizations may well have jumped on the bandwagon and given such functions a new badge without any real change in behaviours, many others are clearly determined to realize genuine insights. This can be achieved in two ways. First there are those 'eureka' moments or flashes of inspiration that can result in specific opportunities being created; and such moments can of course arrive after studying data and analysing research.

However, the second and more germane definition is concerned with the depth of knowledge and understanding of consumer markets that facilitates thinking, planning and decision making about those markets. This is therefore more about the attitudes and skill set of the individual, and arguably these should be finely tuned in all those involved in marketing. One manifestation of these attitudes and skills should be a desire to embrace, and an ability to make sense of, data from a panoply of sources. This will of course include market research studies and customer databases, but should also encompass competitor intelligence, feedback from the sales force and customer service teams, financial performance, and data about complaints from customers.

The resultant picture of the consumer emanating from this activity should therefore cover, over and above the harder factual data of what people buy, when and where they buy it, the 'softer' aspects taking in the influences on these decisions such as media activity, the actions of competitors, as well as customers' experiences, aspirations and expectations. Given that not all sources of data will necessarily point in the same direction, there is a premium on the ability to weigh the information and make sense of it all by giving due emphasis to the more important elements.

Given the diversity of information sources required to make up a complete picture, it is also inevitable that different functional areas in the same organization will be involved. In larger organizations sometimes the one thing that is not in place is a structure for bringing this information together. This is why it should be a more deep-rooted requirement that transcends any structural issues within the organization; and so much more than a rebadging exercise for an existing function.

THE EVOLUTION OF A DISCIPLINE – HR

Back in the 1970s HR (as it almost certainly was not called then) will primarily be remembered for its involvement in industrial relations. In the UK, trade union membership peaked at 12.6 million people, or over half the working population (the figure is now less than a third). The decade had begun with the Industrial Relations Act of 1971, which was subsequently repealed following a change of government and replaced by the Trade Union and Labour Relations Act of 1974. However, the climate was such that unemployment rose to levels that were considered unacceptable, and strike action by several major trade unions helped bring down the Labour government in 1979 following the so-called 'winter of discontent'.

At the same time there were still HR functions that displayed signs of being largely concerned with employee welfare. This was particularly true of service industries that still operated on the basis of offering careers from entry through to retirement. Indeed, in banking, at that time perhaps the apotheosis (outside the public sector) of the lifetime career, the usual name was still the 'staff department', so even the graduation to 'personnel' was yet to happen. Despite, and possibly because of, this the function was an extremely influential one, capable of either realizing or dashing employees' career aspirations.

Whichever characteristics the HR function displayed, from dispensing welfare through to negotiating pay and conditions, the relationship between the individual and the organization was weighted heavily towards the latter. Individuals were much more dependent on the organization than vice versa, as the concept of moving between employers was much less developed than it has now become, and the psychological contract was a quite different entity (see below).

By the 21st century many changes had occurred which transformed the role and remit of what had become the HR (and sometimes human capital or talent) function. Gone are the days of the paternalistic employer (except in smaller, independent businesses), where the personnel function may have adopted the role of employee advocate. Equally, it is not enough for HR staff to just be legal and administrative experts, essential though these elements are given the increasing legislative burden on business and the vital necessity of ensuring that the business has enough people, all of whom get paid when they expect to be paid.

The HR function has also become much more aligned to the goals of the business, as the value of the resource that is represented by people has become truly appreciated, and this has been happening at the same time as the old psychological contracts that tied people into their employer have been broken. Careers are clearly no longer cradle to grave, and employees operate in a way that is much closer to the model of the customer who picks and chooses where purchases are made. Loyalty is no longer something that can be taken for granted, but has to be earned and maintained over the long term by virtue of the organization's ability to develop an offer that meets the continuing and changing needs of the customer or the employee.

BUSINESS GOALS

In some ways the notion of the HR function acting in a strategic fashion is simply good practice whereby it ensures that all of its policies and activities are complementary or congruent. There is clearly little point in offering a world-class package of benefits if the recruitment processes are not in place to ensure that the best candidates become aware of this and are selected if they apply. Similarly the best-intentioned performance management and reward systems that focus on the individual can seriously frustrate aspirations to promote a team-based culture.

In order to take things to the next level, HR functions are seeking to operate in such a way that they inform decision making and are not simply the implementers of decisions made elsewhere. The constraints of the internal and external labour markets are taken into account when determining how the business will develop, and are not issues that are realized belatedly after the strategy has been set.

THE PSYCHOLOGICAL CONTRACT

This phrase has been attributed to Chris Argyris, who first wrote about it in 1960 and sought to use it as a means of analysing employer and employee expectations. A definition offered by Guest and Conway (2002) is 'the perceptions of the two parties, employee and employer, of what their mutual obligations are towards each other'. It is therefore the sum of interactions which can predate the commencement of employment and will almost certainly include a set of expectations established during the recruitment process. Thereafter the contract will evolve as further events unfold, promises are made (and kept or broken) and actions are taken. This will occur at the personal level, for example in appraisals, but can also happen at a corporate level, such that a group of individuals or the entire organization is affected by a decision.

In contrast to the typical document presented as a contract of employment, which may end up being tested in a court or tribunal, the psychological contract is not something that can be enforced legally. From the viewpoint of the employer it is more of a guide to how employees are expected to behave, in return for which they can expect certain things out of their employment.

As with consumer brands, trust is a very strong component of the contract, and if damaged it requires a considerable effort to repair. In addition, other values such as consistency (over time as well as between individuals) are extremely important, along with how the deal between employee and employer is manifest or delivered in reality.

In a virtuous circle of trust and successful delivery it is to be expected that job satisfaction and commitment to the organization will rise. Conversely, it can easily turn into a vicious circle as employees respond to failures to deliver. Whether these are corporate or individual failures, they can lead to poor performance and even resignation. An example of a break in the psychological contract at the corporate level that has occurred in several sectors has been the move away from lifetime careers. People who entered the organization on the expectation that they would remain there throughout their working lives can find themselves subject to potential redundancy at a time in their career when it might not be possible to get a job elsewhere.

THE EMPLOYER BRAND

In the same way that the concept of a successful brand in marketing and business embodies all manifestations and points of contact between a customer or potential customer and that organization, so the same organization should be managing in a cohesive manner all those points of contact that employees and prospective employees may have with it.

Simon Barrow succinctly summarized the employer brand concept in 'Understanding people at work – a new priority for researchers?' (1996):

> The employer brand consists of all those factors which affect how people feel about their work. Physical factors like the conditions in which they work, the location of their job, how they are paid, how they are managed, how they are assessed, trained and developed. What their peer group is like. How they feel about the organization and its aim.

In the same way that a successful consumer brand is built upon qualities such as recognition, consistency and trust, the same is true of an employer brand; it is simply that the 'consumer' of employment is buying a different type of package of goods and services from those supplied to the world at large. In many respects the concept of the employer brand is in itself a development from the psychological contract, representing an attempt to codify it and be more specific about what the organization has to offer employees.

EMPLOYEE INSIGHT

What is particularly interesting about the concept of the employer brand is that it represents the coming together of the HR and marketing disciplines. For so long HR simply looked after employee issues, almost in isolation, while marketing managed the customer dimension. Yet the growing importance of people to business success has assisted the realization that business policy and goals should be informed by HR as much as HR is dictated by them. In turn, HR can benefit from the skills and disciplines developed within the marketing arena, notably in communication (to inform) and research and analysis (to learn from the workforce).

Many HR functions have long had large amounts of data about employees. What they may not have had, as it would not previously have been considered a core skill, is the analytical expertise or indeed the technology to fully exploit this data. In addition, as with the development of customer insight, there has to be a desire to embrace a wide range of data sources, which again may not traditionally have been in the province of HR. In particular it is important to supplement the factual data held about people with information about attitudes, preferences and expectations. This will not only assist in defining what the employment offer should be, but will help determine the way in which it should be communicated.

So in the same way that consumer marketing techniques are deployed to increase brand loyalty, improve customer satisfaction and profitability, HR can seek to increase employee loyalty, improve employee satisfaction and efficiency through more effective use of resources. For example, the improvement in satisfaction and loyalty should necessitate lower recruitment costs as turnover rates are reduced. Moreover the strength of the organization's image and reputation as an employer will make the task of recruiting the best candidates that much easier.

In addition, if the employment proposition is integrated into the overall brand strategy there should be a greater consistency between the offers to customers and to employees, with the additional benefits derived from greater customer satisfaction and loyalty.

HOW THIS INSIGHT HAPPENS

At the simplest, insights can be derived from intelligent analysis and interpretation of single data sources. Beyond this the growing use of combinations of quantitative and qualitative research methodologies in employee studies offers tremendous synergies, as the one helps inform and explain the other. Previous chapters have discussed the merits and applications of the two broad types of research. Yet the deeper understanding of people comes from sensitive use of both, so that each provides the contribution that is best suited to it.

Perhaps the biggest potential will be derived from combining the outputs of research studies with data from other sources. Primarily within the HR function, but often elsewhere in an organization, such as in finance and line management, there is usually a wealth of data about individuals, which if harnessed contributes towards a holistic view of any one employee.

Even with all of the existing information aggregated to form a view of an individual, there will still be relevant information that has not been collected. An example of such information could be the leisure interests of employees. Although not directly relevant to performance at work, it is the sort of information that helps to describe and understand the employee as a person. As was noted in earlier chapters there are many employees who become involved in community activities because of a personal interest and not as part of any formal programme sponsored by their employer. Knowledge of these activities could help the organization to understand attitudes towards reward, career development and working hours, for instance.

There are obviously implications if such additional data is not seen to be central to the organization, not least in terms of the resources that would need to be devoted to collecting and storing it. Here research can help, as it may form part of a survey that feeds directly into a segmentation analysis, or can be linked through data fusion techniques (see later in this chapter).

Attention also needs to be paid to the prevailing data protection legislation. In the UK this means that the obligations that are pertinent are those that require the data to be obtained for specified and lawful purposes; that the data should be adequate, relevant and not excessive for these purposes; and that it should be accurate, kept up to date and not kept longer than is necessary.

Without contravening this legislation, or the confidence in which certain information about an employee is held, it is important to consider that frequently in their relationships with employees (as well as customers), organizations fail to demonstrate they possess knowledge about an individual which that individual believes the organization has. Hence efforts should be made to gather the information known about any employee and to ensure that it is available to be used for the benefit of him or her.

In addition to the data that is recorded by an organization about an employee as a person, a further source of insight comes from other people outside the organization with whom employees interact on behalf of their employer, notably customers. Such feedback may be at the level of teams rather than individuals, but it is still very informative if it helps substantiate the true value of an employee to an organization.

In essence there is a case for using a variation of the balanced business scorecard approach (see Chapter 1) in assessing and developing individual employees holistically. The learning and growth perspective is relevant to individuals' capacity and desire to develop and hence their potential, while the business process perspective can be adapted to deal with the efficiency and effectiveness of job performance. Even though not all employees will deal with external customers directly, the customer perspective can be populated by feedback gathered from internal customers as well as a more general assessment of the indirect contribution made to customer satisfaction. Although the financial perspective may also sometimes be lacking measures such as the income or profit directly attributable to an individual, it nevertheless is appropriate to consider the employment costs of individuals against the overall contribution they make.

Before we discuss some of the other techniques used to generate insights that have not previously been covered in this book, it is appropriate to consider the development of HR information systems (HRIS) and the extent to which they can contribute to the body of knowledge held by an organization about its workforce.

HR Information Systems (HRIS)

The development of the HR function has gone hand in hand with an exploitation of the potential of IT systems. Often HR systems had their origins in handling the payroll. These days it is more common to find that they not only handle broader aspects of reward but also take in sickness and other absences, training and development, diversity and performance management.

As a study by the CIPD (2004) showed, the extent to which broader aspects, such as expenses and communication, are part of an organization-wide system will depend on the integration of systems generally within an organization. Even though the average age of the systems covered by the study was four years, only a quarter of the organizations indicated that their HRIS was integrated in any way with their other systems.

The principal benefits that organizations expected to gain from introducing such systems were improving the quality of information, and the speed at which it was made available. It was also deemed important that the system reduced the administrative burden on the HR department. Happily, for the majority of organizations these expectations had been realized.

Nevertheless there were significant numbers responding to the survey that intended to target integration as a key requirement when existing systems were scheduled to be developed or replaced. The primary reason that it had not happened already appeared to be concerned with pragmatic decisions about the timing and amount of expenditure, since few organizations opt to introduce systems across different areas at the same time. This then requires considerable effort and expense in aligning systems after the event.

While the full integration of systems will facilitate the type of data-mining techniques used in consumer marketing to maximize the understanding available to the organization, other research techniques and analytical skills will continue to play a part in generating insights.

Key driver analysis

Key driver analysis uses linear regression techniques to assist in the interpretation of data. It has been used extensively in the analysis of results from surveys concerned with such matters as customer satisfaction. The approach has also been readily used in employee research, and as with any other application it requires data from a substantial and statistically representative sample. The values given by the respondents to a measure of, say, job satisfaction are then treated as the dependent variable (in mathematical terms).

Those factors that might be expected to contribute towards variations in the level of job satisfaction between different employees are classified as independent variables. In an employee survey the sort of factors that might be examined are opportunities for training and development, recognition, teamworking, openness and communication, and qualities exhibited by managers and supervisory staff.

The analysis that takes place ascribes weights or coefficients to these independent variables, from which those that have the greatest impact can readily be determined. In addition the analysis will calculate the cumulative effect of all the independent variables. This is important to identify whether the sum total of these variables explains a small or large fraction of the variations in job satisfaction, and hence whether there may be other significant factors not included in the modelling. The process can also eliminate any duplication between independent variables that are highly correlated with each other and so do not add anything to the overall explanation.

Although the techniques used to perform the analysis demand an understanding of mathematics and statistics, the outputs can readily be presented in a graphical form to highlight the impact and relative importance of the variables analysed for a wider audience.

Segmentation

Segmentation can take many forms and has long been used as a strategic tool in marketing. Essentially it recognizes that not all customers are the same, and it is more efficient to identify sub-groups whose needs and wants are homogeneous, though distinct from those of other segments. There is also an expectation that the different segments will respond to different communications specifically targeted at them.

In order for any approach to segmentation to be effective there are some fundamental criteria that the segments need to meet. First of all the characteristics that define a segment must be readily identifiable and capable of being measured. It will not be much help if it is not possible to collect the relevant information from people, or if the importance of the segment that they represent cannot be measured in some way.

Once the size of a segment has been determined, it will only be worth pursuing if it is substantial and merits specific attention over and above anything that might be produced for the general population. This in turn assumes that there is adequate differentiation between segments, and that each is capable of being reached through targeted communications.

There are a variety of ways in which a market can be segmented, and most of these have their potential counterparts in employee studies. The most common relate to demographics, which in consumer terms are primarily concerned with age or life-stage, socioeconomic class, level of educational achievement, location lived in and so on. In employee terms age and/or length of service, grade or status and place of work (either physically or in an organizational structure chart) are the comparable factors which are frequently used in any analysis of attitudes and behaviour.

The benefit of segmenting employees in these ways is that it is readily achieved by gathering the relevant details as part of a survey and ensuring that the specification of the outputs from the survey groups the responses of each segment together. Comparisons between the segments can then be read from the data tables. The limitation of this approach is that it is primarily descriptive of a situation, and leads only as far as suggesting hypotheses which then need to be tested, rather than providing explanations why a given result has occurred.

Consequently other forms of segmentation have been developed in consumer markets that seek to go beyond description and explain why, for instance, people make the purchases they do. These forms of segmentation are therefore characterized by being based on the needs of consumers, the benefits they derive from the purchases they make, their lifestyles and so on.

When considering the relationship between employee and employer the equivalent analysis would help to explain why people choose the type of work they do or the particular organization they work for. By way of an example, it might be expected that those who wish to work for charitable organizations do not expect relatively high salaries. An analysis designed to verify this would inevitably have to take in employees from a broad spectrum of organizations, and is probably beyond the resources of any single organization.

A further segmentation approach that is readily applicable within an organization usually comes under the heading of attitudinal or psychographics, as it is more concerned with psychological traits. As with segmentations based on needs and benefits, there is recognition that people who, say, live in the same place or are the same age can hold quite different attitudes and/or behave quite differently. The segmentation therefore seeks to identify the characteristics of those who hold similar views, with the intention of meeting their particular requirements.

Since many employee opinion surveys already consist of a wealth of attitudinal data, there is tremendous potential to undertake this sort of analysis. Typically, the approach combines the use of the statistical techniques called factor analysis and cluster analysis. The former identifies the broad attitude dimensions underlying the responses to the statements in the questionnaire (for example, those statements respondents are asked to agree or disagree with).

In seeking to determine those factors that provide the greatest explanation for variations in attitudes held, it is possible that the process will generate alternative solutions, say, with varying numbers of factors in them. Sound judgement is then required in selecting the solution to be taken forward since, as with any form of segmentation, it ultimately has to make sense to those who are going to work with it.

Here it can be helpful to have undertaken some prior qualitative research in which the moderator has interviewed a cross-section of employees and been able to generate hypotheses about potentially different segments based on the variations in attitudes held. Such inputs not only provide a basis from which to select the appropriate solution, they also add colour and richness to the mathematical outputs of the factor analysis.

Based on these outputs it is then possible to perform the cluster analysis which is used to identify those groups of respondents with shared attitudes. Again an element of judgement is required as, for instance, the number of clusters or groupings generated by the statistical procedure could include one or more that represent very small proportions of the workforce. Re-running the analysis to eliminate these may provide a solution that can be implemented more effectively even if it does not provide the greatest mathematical separation.

Once robust clusters have been identified, it is then helpful to generate portraits of these employee types and label them so as to bring the segmentation 'alive'. Although segments will never be as different as black and white, it is still critical to identify the darker shades of grey by highlighting more definite attitudes towards different topics, or other characteristics that are more evident in some than others. One of the dilemmas here is that the premise of the segmentation is that attitudes vary within demographic categories; yet segments can be more recognizable if it is possible to say that one is, say, older and another is younger, or one is more likely to be found in a particular region or division.

However, even without the ability to describe segments based on attitudes in a neat and tidy fashion, the organization still has information that supports the need to tailor its communications to different groups in different ways. To a certain extent, assuming that the communications are broadcast, these groups will self-select those messages that resonate with them.

CASE STUDY

An example of an organization that has undertaken this type of analysis is Tesco. A much admired company and readily acknowledged as the leading retailer in the UK (and increasingly in other parts of the world), Tesco has built its success on its marketing skills. One particular example is the way in which it harnessed the power of its customer database when it launched its loyalty card, the Clubcard. Through the knowledge acquired in this way about the shopping habits of its customers it could pinpoint developments that would increase their expenditure at its stores.

In addition, according to a report 'Employee as customer: lessons from marketing and IT' by Dr Mark Dorgan (2003), Tesco has analysed the demographics and preferences of its employees across stores and functions, and segmented them into five groups: 'want it all', 'work–life balancers', 'pleasure seekers', 'live to work' and 'work to live'. These classifications recognize the different expectations that employees have from a job or career at the company. This means that Tesco can tailor the offer it makes, in terms of such things as the work environment, the hours of work, the pay and benefits or the career paths.

This application of approaches to employees similar to those practised for the benefit of customers is typified by a quote from David Fairhurst, Group Resourcing Director at Tesco. At a Recruitment Society event on 14 September 2004 (reported on Tesco's website) he said that the 'magic formula' could be illustrated through the equation: $L^2 (c + e) + r = s + p$. 'That means: listening a lot to our customers and employees plus responding accordingly equals sales and profitability,' he said.

To make the formula work, organizations must also learn to raise employee engagement through effective line leadership. Fairhurst went on to say that 'Leadership is about treating people as individuals – treating your employees the same way you treat your customers.'

Data fusion

In contrast to the notion of integrating information systems, whereby all of the data relating to one person is available at one point, data fusion seeks to combine the data about one person from multiple sources. In consumer marketing attempts are often made to combine customer data held by the organization with data from a market research survey. More sophisticated attempts at fusion seek to populate a database by matching records of similar rather than the same people, with the aim of generating a larger dataset. In part this reflects the fact that samples in market research are often a small fraction of the size of internal customer databases.

With employee data, the total population is normally more manageable, while often surveys are conducted among a high proportion of the total workforce. Therefore the concept of matching records for the same person is more feasible, and this is therefore the concern of this section.

It is recognized that fusing data records for employees, in the same way as described above for customers, is not a straightforward matter. The primary limitation on such activities stems from the sensitivities regarding confidentiality of information and the data protection legislation. It is of paramount importance that those being asked to take part in a survey are made aware in advance what will happen to the information they provide. Therefore accessing such data after the survey and using it for a different purpose such as fusion is not condoned.

In consumer research, there are further sensitivities such that the processing in any fusion exercise will be undertaken by the external research company, so it is not possible for the client organization to access the information provided by the customers. Equally, the reverse may be true with employee records, as there may be restrictions on what employee data can be passed on to a third party by the employer.

Set against these sensitivities is the fact that for many organizations the data they hold about employees is incomplete, and there is a lack of integration between various systems holding the data that is known. There is therefore a role for research to supplement the known data, and consideration needs to be given to obtaining the necessary permissions and taking the precautions required so that a full and thorough analysis can be undertaken combining various data sources.

CONCLUSIONS

There is every indication that research among employees is now being accorded an importance that matches the importance of employees to an employer. As the employment balance becomes more even, so it becomes critical for an organization to have an understanding of its workforce that matches the understanding it has of its markets and customers.

Not only can research supplement the internal data sources about employees, the skill set of researchers means that the analysis and interpretation of the combined information can yield genuine insights for the benefit of all concerned.

This means that the full range of research techniques should be exploited and harnessed, with the aim of enhancing the understanding that any organization has of its workforce, their aspirations and expectations.

Appendix 1: Information and Consultation Regulations

INTRODUCTION

Legislation around the world that is concerned with communication between employers and employees tends to concentrate on the role of representatives, notably trade unions, and hence is more likely to apply to those who choose to be represented in this way. It is less common to find legislation that is concerned with the relationship and communications between an employer and the totality of the workforce engaged by that organization. The EU Directive dealing with Information and Consultation is one such piece of legislation, embracing the workforce irrespective of whether they are currently represented in any way.

It is therefore legislation that is strongly supported by those involved with representing workers, but it can also be seen to encourage what is arguably in any case good practice in consultation on matters affecting employment in an organization. Consequently it is the type of legislation that could well be enacted in other parts of the world following its implementation across the European Union.

Since the directive and the regulations that flow from it provide a framework for discussion between an organization and the workforce, it touches on many aspects central to this book. Without seeking to be a definitive guide on the legislation (which warrants a book in its own right), this discussion deals with the background, considers some of the formalities and then discusses those aspects of interest and relevance to the broader context of communication within an organization. Specifically the discussion points of interest are:

- employees and representatives;
- content of negotiated agreements;
- information and consultation;
- timing and frequency.

BACKGROUND

Although the ancestry of these regulations can be traced back much further, the immediate origin is to be found in Directive 2002/14/EC of the European Parliament and of the Council of 11 March 2002. This sought to establish a general framework for informing and consulting employees in the European Union. These regulations are being implemented in Great Britain in stages such that they have applied to the largest undertakings (those with 150-plus employees) since 6 April 2005. For undertakings with between 100 and 150 employees the regulations apply from April 2007; whilst in the case of the smallest undertakings covered (those with 50-plus employees) the relevant date is April 2008. The definition of undertaking is generally regarded as one that is carrying out an economic activity, but not necessarily for gain, so it can cover organizations in the public sector as well as those in the private sector. In terms of companies, the definition relates to legal entities rather than an organizational entity such as a division, unit or department, although it is possible for agreements to be established which reflect such organizational structures.

The intention of the regulations is to provide employees with rights to be informed and consulted about the business they work for, including the prospects for employment, and substantial changes in work organization or contractual relations. The requirement does not operate automatically. It is triggered either by a formal request from employees for an information and consultation agreement, or by employers starting the statutory process themselves.

Essentially, the philosophy behind the regulations is concerned with improving dialogue and promoting trust within undertakings. They should make employees more aware of the pressures and situations that could impact on employment in the organization, and it is anticipated that as a result any adverse consequences can be offset and the employability and adaptability of the workforce increased.

The way in which the regulations have been drafted also allows a considerable degree of flexibility in interpretation on issues that may require clarification by the courts or the Central Arbitration Committee (the permanent independent body that adjudicates on disputes between trade unions and employers and the operation of European Works Councils in Great Britain).

Finally, it should be noted that the regulations supplement, and do not replace, existing legislation. By way of an example, the procedures for handling collective redundancies set out in the Trade Union and Labour Relations (Consolidation) Act 1992 apply irrespective of any agreements reached under the Information and Consultation Regulations. These latter agreements come with the shorthand description of ICE, standing for information and consultation of employees.

FORMALITIES AND SOME PARAMETERS

The flexibility that characterizes these regulations inevitably makes it more difficult to encapsulate all of the steps and possible outcomes in a simple flowchart. The flowchart that follows therefore is not exhaustive, but is a schematic representation of the major issues facing organizations as they approach the subject for the first time.

The principal considerations are:

- The capacity of either the employers or employees to initiate the process designed to lead to an agreement.
- A request from employees must be in writing and dated. The significance of the date is that it acts as the point of reference for the size of the workforce, and hence the number needed to be in support of the request, as well as the timeframe for the process that follows.
- Whether there is a prior agreement that matches the obligations imposed by the regulations.
- In the absence of such a 'pre-existing' agreement or an initiative by the employers, the proportion of the workforce required to support negotiations that would lead to an agreement is 10 per cent.
- Where there is a pre-existing agreement, the proportion needed to support negotiations for a fresh agreement rises to 40 per cent.
- To be valid a pre-existing agreement must be in writing and not simply be a matter of custom and practice.
- It must also cover all employees and have been approved, by means of a ballot, through an expression supported by signatures, or the agreement of employee representatives acting on behalf of a majority of the workforce.

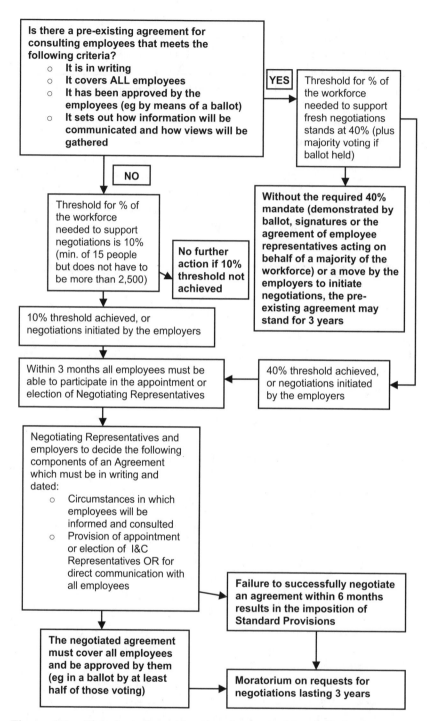

Figure A1 *Flowchart of considerations in approaching the Information and Consultation Regulations*

- Finally, in keeping with the regulations the pre-existing agreement must set out how the employer will provide information to and consult with the workforce.

Interestingly, given the heritage of this legislation and the philosophy behind works councils, an agreement under the European Works Council (EWC) Directive is unlikely to be valid as a pre-existing agreement given that the focus of European Works Councils is on transnational issues. Indeed, the Information and Consultation Regulations have been described as the 'national works council' law to differentiate it from the EWC legislation.

The regulations provide for two types of representative. The first type covers those that are appointed or elected to negotiate on behalf of the workforce, once support for negotiations has been established. The second category will then act on behalf of the workforce under the terms of the agreement once it has been reached. The relevance of these representatives is such that their position is considered in more detail later, although for the time being it is important to stress that the same people will not necessarily fulfil both roles.

Another critical aspect concerns the time limits contained within the regulations. Once an agreement has been reached the principle is that there should be a three-year moratorium on requests to initiate the process again. The rationale for such a moratorium is that it prevents one party unilaterally seeking to unwind the agreement that was successfully negotiated.

This area also provides a good example of the flexibility that has been incorporated into the legislation, and how the mutual consent of employers and employees can transcend what is prescribed in the regulations. Here, by agreement they can overturn the prescribed duration of a three-year moratorium and fresh negotiations can take place within a shorter timeframe. Similarly, if negotiations are taking longer than the nominal six months this timeframe can be extended by mutual agreement.

Failure to negotiate an agreement can result in the imposition of the Standard Provisions contained in the Regulations. Not only would this mean the loss of flexibility over what can be contained in the agreement, it also affects other elements that might be included in it such as the election of representatives.

DISCUSSION POINTS

Employees and representatives

Employees

An apparently simple piece of information, the total number of employees in the undertaking, is clearly an important reference point for these regulations, in determining who is to be covered by an agreement or the number required to meet a threshold of support, for instance. Consequently there are specific provisions to ensure that requests to be informed of this are met, such that a request that is in writing and is dated must be answered within one month.

The regulations provide a reminder, if any were necessary, of the continuing absence of a firm definition of what constitutes an employee. For those who are considering any form of exercise whereby they wish to involve the workforce and are unclear who should be covered, here is a reprise of the more successful tests devised by the courts over the years:

- Does the person have to undertake the work personally? While a limited power to substitute another person in his or her place has been held not to be necessarily incompatible with being an employee, the more freedom someone has to do so, the less likely he or she is to be an employee.
- What level of control does the employer have over the person? Although this test may not always fit the case of, say, skilled or professional people, when the employer might not have the necessary expertise to really control the workers and they are left to undertake their work as they see fit, generally it is deemed that the likelihood of being an employee increases with the degree of control exercised by the employer.
- Are there any other factors in the relationship which would be incompatible with the contract being one of employment? Again this test is not always conclusive but a good example relates to the use of equipment provided by the employer. Where people use their own equipment (such as tools and materials), the contract with the employer will seem less like one of employment.

When assessing the total number of employees, or deciding who to involve in a research or communications exercise, it would therefore be usual to exclude subcontractors as well as those such as temporary agency workers who typically do not have a contract of employment with the undertaking.

Interestingly, for the purpose of counting the total number of employees (and hence determining the size of the undertaking) part-time employees can be counted as though they were full-time employees, although the employer may opt to count them as representing half a full-time employee if they worked under a contract for 75 hours or less in any month during the relevant period. However, when it comes to a ballot (for example to approve an agreement or elect a representative), part-time employees must be treated in an identical fashion to full-time employees.

Another stipulation regarding the total number of employees is that it is based on the average number of employees over the preceding 12-month period. The impact of this can be seen in organizations involved in seasonal activities, such that the total number employed at the time of the request would be significantly different from the average over the previous year (arrived at by totalling the numbers employed each month and dividing the total by 12).

Representatives

Under the regulations, as has been noted previously, there are two types of employee representatives: those who negotiate the agreement that will cover how employees are informed and consulted, and those who act as information and consultation (I&C) representatives under the terms of the negotiated agreement.

Representatives involved in negotiating the agreement can be appointed or elected, but all the employees of the undertaking are entitled to take part in such appointments or elections. In addition, during the subsequent negotiations, all employees of the undertaking must be represented. This in turn may influence the number of representatives, something that is not specified in the regulations.

As part of the agreement, as has been noted, there can be provision for informing and consulting with the workforce directly. In practice, certainly in larger organizations, there is likely to be a role for I&C representatives. The number of I&C representatives can be agreed by the parties, as can the method of appointment or election, along with the length of time they will serve for and how they may be replaced.

The specification of the standard provisions is that the number of these representatives should be proportional to the number of employees in the undertaking: one per 50 employees or part thereof, subject to a minimum of two representatives and a maximum of 25. In other words, this suggests that there should be two representatives for undertakings with 50 to 100 employees, three for those with 101 to 150 employees and so on.

It is also worth adding that the number should reflect the diversity of the workforce. Apart from the geographic and demographic make-up, there could well be a number of different working practices (such as shift patterns of functional areas) that would make it appropriate for each group to have its own representative.

Content of negotiated agreements

It is explicit in the regulations that it is up to the employer and employees to negotiate the content of the agreement that will govern how information is conveyed and consultation undertaken. However, the following section provides a useful checklist of what negotiated agreements could cover.

■ The undertakings and the staff in those undertakings covered by the agreement, and whether different provisions apply to separate parts of the undertaking (for example individual establishments, divisions or sections of the workforce) although collectively these separate arrangements must cover all the employees of the undertaking.

■ The subject matter to be covered; how those subjects will be chosen and how agendas for meetings will be drawn up.

■ The relationship between the agreement and any collective agreements that are in place with trade unions.

■ The handling of matters governed by other requirements to inform and consult the workforce (such as health and safety law and European Works Councils), so as to avoid any unnecessary duplication of effort.

■ The date and duration of the agreement.

■ Methods, frequency and timing of information and consultation.

■ Whether I&C representatives will be elected or appointed, or the employer intends to inform and consult directly with employees (or a combination thereof), and how this will happen.

■ The number of representatives and any obligations placed upon them to consult with and report back to employees; whether anyone other than an employee can be a representative.

■ How the views and opinions of employees will be gathered, and what the employer will do in response to the expression of these views and opinions.

■ The type and nature of information to be provided to employees and in addition when and how often information will be provided and consultation will take place (for instance whether it will occur on different levels such as local and regional as well as national).

■ The methods for dealing with confidential or price-sensitive information; the obligations placed on those in receipt of such information and any disciplinary measures for those in breach of the obligations.

■ The agreement must also contain procedures providing for the resolution of any disputes.

The agreement, which must be in writing, should then be signed by a person on behalf of the management of the company and approved by the employees. The latter approval can be demonstrated by the document being signed by all the negotiating representatives; or a majority of the negotiating representatives, provided that it is seen to be supported by either 50 per cent of all employees in writing or 50 per cent of those employees voting in a ballot.

Information and consultation

Under the standard provisions of the regulations, information and consultation is deemed to embrace three principal categories.

Information on the recent and probable development of the undertaking's or the establishment's activities and economic situation

Unlike the subsequent categories, there is no requirement to consult on these topics, only to provide information on them. Indeed, there is no requirement for a meeting to take place during which the information is provided. However a meeting might well be sensible in order to explain some of the information, since it must be given in an 'appropriate' fashion, in particular to allow the representatives to conduct an adequate study of it.

The intention is that the information assists in providing I&C representatives with the context in which decisions affecting employment, work organization and employees' contractual relations will be made. The nature and extent of information provided under this heading should sensibly relate to the decisions that could be reached under the other two categories which do involve consultation.

By starting with these latter categories, and focusing on those aspects of the recent and probable development of the undertaking's activities and economic situation that affect employment, work organization and employees' contractual relations within an individual organization, it will be easier to determine which items of information should be provided. Again it is not possible to be prescriptive about such matters given that the factors that influence such outcomes will vary substantially from one organization to another.

To assist with the types of information that could be pertinent (where these developments are likely to affect employment within the undertaking, or lead to substantial changes in work organization or employees' contractual relations) it is first worth considering those that could relate to the undertaking's activities. Here information could be concerned with products or services, launches, significant changes and discontinuations.

Also pertinent will be changes in production capacity or sales levels, as will developments in technology, production processes or ways of working.

Other aspects of probable interest will be restructuring plans, takeovers and mergers, acquisitions and disposals of parts of a business or other assets, investment, and opening or closure of establishments (such as factories or outlets). Likewise reorganizations will be relevant, including a transfer of production or posts to different locations or different divisions/units, as will changes to the undertaking's aims, objectives, vision, mission statement, strategy, business plans or changes in senior management.

Turning to the undertaking's economic situation, the type of information that is likely to be of interest here will be the competitive environment, trading conditions, the outlook for the sector, the level of demand, and the state of the undertaking's order book; along with the undertaking's financial situation based on its accounts.

Information and consultation on the situation, structure and probable development of employment within the undertaking or establishment and on any anticipatory measures envisaged, in particular where there is a threat to employment

The emphasis here is on the overall number of employees in the undertaking, both current and future levels. It would therefore include recruitment of additional employees and redundancies (whether voluntary or compulsory), staff turnover, the possibility of moving to reduced hours working or the need for overtime, and could include changes in retirement policy or early retirement schemes.

Since it also includes the 'structure' of employment, this is understood to mean how employees are distributed within the undertaking, for example, geographically at different establishments (plants, offices, factories, retail outlets, branches), or organizationally within different divisions or units of the undertaking. It would therefore include a reorganization of posts within the undertaking, redeployment of staff, or a transfer of posts to different locations.

Meanwhile 'anticipatory measures envisaged, in particular where there is a threat to employment' are deemed to refer to employee training and skill development so as to increase the 'employability and adaptability' of affected employees. This suggests the employer should consider whether the threat to employment can be offset through redeploying and perhaps retraining employees whose posts are under threat.

Since this category concerns employment as a whole within the undertaking, it is not about individual posts or employees. It does not require information and consultation to take place on the recruitment, redundancy, dismissal, retirement, redeployment, training, development or transfer of an individual employee or of a small number of employees.

It is not possible to specify a lower limit in terms of the number of employees who would have to be affected as this will depend on the circumstances of the individual case. Clearly, the more employees affected, and the greater the proportion of all the employees in the undertaking, the more likely it is to come within this category. A situation that is likely to lead on to collective redundancies as defined by statute (that is, 20 or more redundancies at one establishment) would be covered.

The purpose of consulting I&C representatives on the matters covered by this category is to give them the opportunity to express their views on the existing level and structure of employment within the undertaking, and its probable development, including possible recruitment or redundancies, and any plans to redeploy or retrain affected employees.

Information and consultation on decisions likely to lead to substantial changes in work organization or in contractual relations, including those covered by the Community provisions referred to in Article 9(1) (the directives on collective redundancies and business transfers)

The EU Directive does not specify what the terms 'work organization' and 'contractual relations' are meant to include, other than collective redundancies and business transfers. However, the Department of Trade and Industry (DTI) has offered its views on what these phrases would include.

Regarding changes in work organization, it is felt that these would include changes in the level or distribution of employment within the undertaking, including redundancies, along with changes in policy on flexible working, part-time working and overtime. In addition a move to reduced hours or overtime working, and changes in shift working or other work patterns would also be covered.

Meanwhile changes in contractual relations would arise should there be a new employer as a result of a transfer of the business, or part of the business. Also relevant would be substantial changes in employees' terms and conditions (including hours of work, leave entitlement, rest breaks) or the introduction of, or a change to, compulsory retirement age. Further changes that would be covered include those to an occupational pension scheme where there is a contractual right to participation in the scheme, as well as changes in disciplinary or grievance procedures. In the DTI's view 'changes in contractual relations' would not cover changes in pay or benefits that have a monetary value.

Overall, the context of the directive is about employment within the undertaking, and it is reasonable to infer that 'contractual relations' mean the employer's contractual relations with employees, rather than a business's contracts with third parties. Since it concerns 'substantial changes' in work organization or contractual relations, this is not about individual posts or employees. Consequently, as with the previous category, it does not cover the recruitment, terms and conditions, redundancy, dismissal and so on of an individual employee or of a small number of employees.

As with the previous category there will be some debate about the number of employees who would have to be affected, which, as ever, will depend on the circumstances of the individual case. Clearly, the more employees affected, and the greater the proportion of all the employees in the undertaking, the more likely it is to come within this category.

Consultation

Given the importance of consultation, over and above the provision of information, it is worth considering this in more detail. In general terms consultation between an employer and employees should be beneficial in terms of the involvement that all parties have and the quality of the decision making that ensues. That said, consultation is also something that can be handled badly with adverse effects if expectations about what can be achieved are mismanaged and there are no discernible outcomes.

This is where the framework that the legislation seeks to provide should be helpful. The regulations define consultation as 'the exchange of views and establishment of dialogue' between the employer and representatives.

Clearly, representatives are expected to be given information in such a manner and such time that they are able to study and consider it in advance of any consultation. These consultations must be an opportunity to express the views and opinions representatives have formed, in discussions with the level of management and representation relevant to the subject under discussion (that is, that part of the management team with the authority to change the decision being consulted about). The representatives are then entitled to a reasoned response from the employer.

Indeed, consultation about the decisions referred to in the third category above (concerned with work organization and contractual relations) must be undertaken 'with a view to reaching agreement' if those decisions are within the scope of the employer's powers. Although this does not mean that there must be agreement on such decisions, it can be argued it is encouraging both parties to reach agreement.

From case law in other contexts it is clear that the person consulting is not obliged to adopt all or any of the views expressed by those being consulted. This means it is not a co-decision by the employer and employee representatives, neither is it negotiation nor bargaining between them. Decision making remains the responsibility of management. However, it is still more than simply providing information, as set out above.

Finally, as has been noted previously, there is no specific obligation for I&C representatives to report back to the employees they represent, or to obtain their views. Nevertheless, it is good practice for them to do so, so that the views of the workforce are fairly represented in meetings with employers.

Timing and frequency

There is no specification in the legislation as to the frequency or timing of information and consultation. These are matters to be discussed and agreed by the parties concerned. However, it is possible to identify some useful pointers in respect of each.

Timing

It has been noted before that information must be provided to representatives in good time so that they can consider it in advance of a meeting called to discuss it. Just how far in advance of the meeting will depend on the quantity and complexity of the information. Another consideration here may be the confidentiality of the information.

Given the requirement to provide information on 'probable developments', the timing of this obviously has to be in advance rather than after the event; but it also must reflect the degree of certainty of the developments, so that they are indeed likely to happen.

Similarly, consultation implies an activity that happens prior to any decision making, such that there is the possibility of influencing that decision. However, it must be borne in mind that consultation can take place at too advanced a stage, when it may simply serve to alarm and concern, while not serving any practical purpose.

Frequency

Given the intention of the directive of strengthening dialogue and promoting mutual trust, improving risk anticipation and promoting employee involvement, there is clearly an expectation that information should be provided and consulted upon regularly (at least annually) rather than in very specific situations.

It is also recognized that the variety of circumstances affecting any undertaking will determine the need for information and consultation in each one. However, the point made above about the timing in relation to 'probable developments' will influence the frequency as well as timing, given the importance of being able to discuss the specifics as events unfold.

Appendix 2:
The Market Research Society Code of Conduct

INTRODUCTION

The Market Research Society (MRS)

With members in more than 70 countries, MRS is the world's largest association representing providers and users of market, social, and opinion research, and business intelligence.

MRS serves both individuals and organisations who identify with its core values of professionalism, excellence, and effectiveness.

It has a diverse membership of individual researchers within agencies, independent consultancies, client-side organisations, the public sector and the academic community – at all levels of seniority and in all job functions.

MRS Company Partners include agencies, suppliers, and buyers of all types and sizes who are committed throughout their organisations to supporting the core MRS values.

All individual members and Company Partners agree to self-regulatory compliance with the MRS Code of Conduct. Extensive advice to support this commitment is provided by MRS through its Codeline service and by publication of a wide range of specialist guidelines on best practice.

MRS offers various qualifications and membership grades, as well as training and professional development resources to support them. It is the official awarding body in the UK for vocational qualifications in market research.

MRS is a major supplier of publications and information services, conferences and seminars, and many other meeting and networking opportunities for researchers.

MRS is 'the voice of the profession' in its media relations and public affairs activities on behalf of professional research practitioners, and aims to achieve the most favourable climate of opinion and legislative environment for research.

THE CODE OF CONDUCT

This edition:

This edition of the Code of Conduct was agreed by MRS to be operative from 1 December 2005.

It is a fully revised version of a self-regulatory Code which has been in existence since 1954.

Who it applies to:

All Members of the MRS must comply with this Code. It applies to all Members, whether they are engaged in consumer, business-to-business, social, opinion, international or any other type of confidential research project.

It applies to all Members irrespective of the sector or methodologies used eg quantitative, qualitative, mystery shopping.

It also applies to MRS Members when conducting non-market research exercises using research techniques eg database building or research projects which are used for purposes other than research. More detail about these activities can be found in the guidelines *Using Research Techniques for Non-Research Purposes* and clause B48.

Additionally MRS Company Partner organisations are required to take steps to ensure that all individuals employed or engaged by them (whether MRS Members or not) comply with this Code as if they were MRS Members.

The purpose of the Code:

The Code of Conduct is designed to support all those engaged in market, social or opinion research in maintaining professional standards.

The Code is also intended to reassure the general public and other interested parties that research is carried out in a professional and ethical manner.

The principles of the Code:

These are the core principles of the MRS Code of Conduct which are based upon the ESOMAR principles (visit www.esomar.org for more details):

1. Market researchers will conform to all relevant national and international laws.
2. Market researchers will behave ethically and will not do anything which might damage the reputation of market research.
3. Market researchers will take special care when carrying out research among children and other vulnerable groups of the population.
4. Respondents' cooperation is voluntary and must be based on adequate, and not misleading, information about the general purpose and nature of the project when their agreement to participate is being obtained and all such statements must be honoured.
5. The rights of respondents as private individuals will be respected by market researchers and they will not be harmed or disadvantaged as the result of cooperating in a market research project.
6. Market researchers will never allow personal data they collect in a market research project to be used for any purpose other than market research.
7. Market researchers will ensure that projects and activities are designed, carried out, reported and documented accurately, transparently, objectively and to appropriate quality.
8. Market researchers will conform to the accepted principles of fair competition.

The structure of the Code:

Section A of the Code sets out general rules of professional conduct.

Section B of the Code sets out more specific rules of professional conduct as they apply in different aspects of research.

The Appendix sets out the ICC/ESOMAR International Code of Marketing and Social Research Practice.

All MRS Members must adhere to the rules in Sections A and B of the Code.

MRS GUIDELINES AND REGULATIONS

A full list of guidelines, which provide additional best practice guidance, appear on the Society's website www.mrs.org.uk. Unless otherwise stated these guidelines are not binding. Binding guidelines currently in force are as follows:

1. MRS guidance on data protection (which has been written and agreed with the regulator, the Information Commissioner's Office) is binding on Members (except those that are published as consultative drafts).
2. MRS *Guidance Note on Prize Draws* which is based on other self-regulatory rules.

MRS regulations, including those for using research techniques for non-research purposes (which are detailed in a separate document), are binding on Members.

MRS Disciplinary Regulations

Under the MRS Disciplinary Regulations, membership may be withdrawn or other disciplinary action taken, if a Member is deemed guilty of unprofessional conduct. This is defined as a Member:

a) being guilty of any act or conduct which, in the opinion of a body appointed by Council, might bring discredit on the profession, the professional body or its Members; or
b) being found by a body appointed by Council to be guilty of any breach of the rules set out in Sections A and/or B of this Code of Conduct; or
c) being found by a body appointed by Council to be guilty of any breach of the provisions set out in any MRS binding guideline laid down from time to time by the Council; or
d) being found by a body appointed by Council to be guilty of any breach of any other regulations laid down from time to time by Council; or
e) failing without good reason to assist the professional body in the investigation of a complaint; or
f) in the absence of mitigating circumstances having become bankrupt or having made any arrangement or composition with his/her creditors; or
g) being found to be in breach of the Data Protection Act 1998 or other comparable legislation applicable outside the UK. Or being found, by a body appointed by Council, to have infringed any of the eight data protection principles set out in the Act or similar provisions set out in comparable legislation outside the UK.

Note that where more than one MRS Member is involved in a matter under complaint, whilst the MRS reserves the right to proceed with an investigation and other relevant processes against all such Members under its Disciplinary Regulations, it will usually apply its discretion to proceed only against the most senior MRS Member(s) involved.

GENERAL

It is the responsibility of Members to keep themselves updated on changes or amendments to any part of this Code which are published from time to time and announced in publications and on the web pages of the Society. If in doubt about the interpretation of the Code, members may consult the MRS Market Research Standards Board via its Codeline Service which deals with MRS Code enquiries and advises on best practice.

The MRS Code of Conduct does not take precedence over national law. Members responsible for international research shall take its provisions as a minimum requirement and fulfil any other responsibilities set down in law or by nationally agreed standards.

DEFINITIONS FOR THE PURPOSES OF THE MRS CODE OF CONDUCT

Agency:

Agency includes any individual, organisation, department or division, including any belonging to the same organisation as the Client which is responsible for, or acts as, a supplier on all or part of a research project.

Children:

Children are defined as those aged under 16. See Section B for full details about children.

Client:

Client includes any individual, organisation, department or division, including any belonging to the same organisation as the Member, which is responsible for commissioning or applying the results from a research project.

Company Partner:

An organisation with MRS Members that has signed the MRS Company Partner Service Quality Commitment which applies throughout the organisation.

Confidential Research:

Confidential research describes research projects which are for the purposes of research (as defined below) and do not disclose personal details at an identifiable level.

Consultant:

Any individual or organisation that provides research services. Consultants can also be a sub-contractor in the research relationship.

Identity:

The identity of a Respondent includes, as well as his/her name and/or address, any other information which offers a reasonable chance that he/she can be identified by anyone who has access to the information.

Interview:

An interview is any form of contact intended to obtain information from a Respondent or group of Respondents.

Interviewer:

Person involved in the collection of data for market, opinion and social research purposes.

Member:

A Member is an individual who has been admitted to membership of the MRS in one of the five categories set out in Article 3 of the Articles of Association (ie Nominated Members, Full Members, Associate Members, Affiliate Members and Field Members).

Mystery Shopping:

Mystery shopping or Mystery customer research are the same activity and can be defined as: The use of individuals trained to experience and measure any customer service process, by acting as potential customers and in some way reporting back on their experiences in a detailed and objective way.

The Profession:

The profession is the body of research practitioners and others engaged in (or interested in) marketing, social and opinion research.

Professional body:

Professional body refers to MRS.

Public place:

A public place is one to which the public has access (where admission has been gained with or without a charge) and where an individual could reasonably expect to be observed and/or overheard by other people, for example in a shop, in the street or in a place of entertainment.

Publication:

The communication of information to the public.

Records:

The term records includes anything containing information relating to a research project and covers all data collection and data processing documents, audio and visual recordings. Primary records are the most comprehensive record of information on which a project is based; they include not only the original data records themselves, but also anything needed to evaluate those records, such as quality control documents. Secondary records are any other records about the Respondent and the research results.

Recruiter:

Person who identifies and invites Respondents to participate in a research project.

Research:

Research is the collection and analysis of data from a sample or census of individuals or organisations relating to their characteristics, behaviour, attitudes, opinions or possessions. It includes all forms of market, opinion and social research such as consumer and industrial surveys, psychological investigations, qualitative interviews and group discussions, observational, ethnographic, and panel studies.

Respondent:

A Respondent is any individual or organisation from or about whom data is collected or is approached for interview.

Responsible Adult:

An individual who has personal accountability for the well-being of a child, for example a parent, guardian, teacher, nanny or grandparent. See Section B for full details about children.

Sub-contractor:

Any individual or organisation that undertakes a part of a research project under the instruction of the Member (self-employed interviewers are not defined as sub-contractors for the purpose of this Code).

INTRODUCTION TO SECTIONS A AND B

Sections A and B below set out rules of professional conduct.

Section A sets out general rules.

Section B sets out more specific rules as they apply in different aspects of research.

All rules set out in Sections A and B must be observed and adhered to by all MRS Members with any involvement, or with any responsibility, at any level in a matter. This means that more than one MRS Member might be in breach of a rule in respect of the same matter.

Note that where more than one MRS Member is involved in a matter under complaint, whilst the MRS reserves the right to proceed with an investigation and other relevant processes against all such Members under its Disciplinary Regulations, it will usually apply its discretion to proceed only against the most senior MRS Member(s) involved.

All MRS Members should be aware that if found under the MRS Disciplinary Regulations to be in breach of any of the rules in Sections A and/or B of this Code, he/she will be deemed guilty of unprofessional conduct and disciplinary action may be taken against him/her.

For further information about the MRS disciplinary procedure, MRS Members are referred to the relevant section in the Introduction to this Code and to the Disciplinary Regulations themselves (which are available on www.mrs.org.uk).

Participants in the MRS Company Partner Service are also required, in accordance with the terms of the Service, to take steps to ensure that the Code of Conduct is adhered to by all individuals employed or engaged by them (whether MRS Members or not). (The rules of this service are detailed in the Company Partner Quality Commitment.)

SECTION A: GENERAL RULES OF PROFESSIONAL CONDUCT

A1 Research must conform to the national and international legislation relevant to a given project including in particular the Data Protection Act 1998 or other comparable legislation applicable outside the UK.

A2 Members must take reasonable steps to avoid conflicts of interest with Clients or employers and must make prior voluntary and full disclosure to all parties concerned of all matters that might give rise to such conflict.

A3 Members must act honestly in dealings with Respondents, Clients (actual or potential), employers, employees, sub-contractors and the general public.

A4   The use of letters after an individual's name to indicate membership of MRS is permitted only in the case of Fellows (FMRS), Full Members (MMRS) and Associate Members (AMRS). These letters must not be used by any individual not admitted in any of these MRS categories of membership.
Comment: All MRS members may point out, where relevant, that they belong to the appropriate category of the professional body.

A5   Members must not speak or imply that they speak on behalf of MRS unless they have the written authority of Council or of some duly delegated individual or committee.

A6   Members must not make false claims about their skills and experience or those of their organisation.

A7   Members must take reasonable steps to ensure that others do not breach or cause a breach of this Code.
Comment: This includes:
Members taking reasonable steps to ensure that the people with whom they work (including other Members, non-member research practitioners, colleagues, Clients, consultants, sub-contractors) are sufficiently familiar with this Code that they are unlikely to breach or cause it to be breached unknowingly or unintentionally, and
Members with responsibility for implementing processes, procedures and contracts, taking reasonable steps to ensure that they are such that this Code is unlikely to be breached or caused to be breached by others unknowingly or unintentionally.

A8   Members must not act in a way which might bring discredit on the profession, MRS or its Members.

A9   Members must not disparage or unjustifiably criticise other Members or other non-member researchers.

A10 Members must take all reasonable precautions to ensure that Respondents are not harmed or adversely affected as a result of participating in a research project.

SECTION B: RULES OF PROFESSIONAL CONDUCT APPLICABLE TO RESEARCH

This section relates to specific aspects of work commonly carried out by MRS Members and other research practitioners.

Some of the rules in this section are legal requirements. Members should be aware that this Code does not cover all relevant legislative requirements of Members and it is the responsibility of all Members to familiarise themselves with these. Members should be aware in particular that breaches of the Data Protection Act 1998 or other comparable legislation outside the UK are grounds for disciplinary action under MRS Disciplinary Regulations.

Designing and Setting up a Research Project

B1 Members must not knowingly take advantage, without permission, of the unpublished work of another research practitioner which is the property of that other research practitioner.
Comment: This means, where applicable, that Members must not knowingly carry out or commission work based on proposals prepared by a research practitioner in another organisation unless permission has been obtained.

B2 All written or oral assurances made by any Member involved in commissioning or conducting projects must be factually correct and honoured by the Member.

B3 Members must take reasonable steps to design research to the specification agreed with the Client.

B4 Members must take reasonable steps to design research which meets the quality standards agreed with the Client.

B5 Members must take reasonable steps to ensure that the rights and responsibilities of themselves and Clients are governed by a written contract and/or internal commissioning contract.

B6 Members must not disclose the identity of Clients or any confidential information about Clients without the Client's permission unless there is a legal obligation to do so.

Use of Client Databases, Lists and Personal Contact Details

B7 Where lists of named individuals are used eg Client databases, the list source must be revealed at an appropriate point in the interview, if requested. This overrides the right to Client anonymity.

Respondents' Rights to Anonymity

B8 The anonymity of Respondents must be preserved unless they have given their informed consent for their details to be revealed or for attributable comments to be passed on.
Comment: Members must be particularly careful if sample sizes are very small (such as in business and employee research) that they do not inadvertently identify organisations or departments and therefore individuals.

B9 If Respondents have given consent for data to be passed on in a form which allows them to be personally identified, Members must:

- demonstrate that they have taken all reasonable steps to ensure that it will only be used for the purpose for which it was collected; and
- fully inform Respondents as to what will be revealed, to whom and for what purpose.

B10 If Respondents request individual complaints or unresolved issues to be passed back to a Client (for example in customer satisfaction research), Members must comply with that request. The comments/issues to be passed back to a Client must be agreed with the Respondent and must not be linked back to any other data or used for any other purpose without the explicit consent of the Respondent.

Re-interviewing Respondents

B11 A follow up interview with a Respondent can be carried out only if the Respondent's permission has been obtained at the previous interview. The only exception to this is re-contact for quality control purposes.

B12 Any re-contact must match the assurances given to Respondents at the time that permission was gained eg when re-contact was to occur, the purpose and by whom.

B13 Respondent details must not be passed on to another third party for research or any other purposes without the prior consent of the Respondent. The only exception to this is if the Client is the Data Controller of the Respondent data.

Designing the Questionnaire

B14 Members must take reasonable steps to ensure all of the following:

- that questions are fit for purpose and Clients have been advised accordingly;
- that the design and content of questionnaires are appropriate for the audience being researched;
- that Respondents are able to answer the questions in a way that reflects the view they want to express;
- that Respondents are not led towards a particular answer;
- that answers are capable of being interpreted in an unambiguous way;
- that personal data collected is relevant and not excessive.

Preparing for Fieldwork

Communicating with Respondents

B15 If there is to be any recording, monitoring or observation during an interview, Respondents must be informed about this both at re-cruitment and at the beginning of the interview.

B16 Members must not knowingly make use of personal data collected illegally.

Fieldwork

B17 Respondents must not be misled when being asked for cooperation to participate in a research project.

B18 A Respondent's right to withdraw from a research project at any stage must be respected.

B19 Members must ensure that Respondents are able to check without difficulty the identity and bona fides of any individual and/or their employer conducting a research project (including any sub-contractors).

B20 For telephone and face-to-face interviews, calls must not be made to a household (local time) before 9 am weekdays and Saturdays, 10 am Sundays or after 9 pm any day, unless by appointment.

B21 Members must ensure that all of the following are clearly communicated to the Respondent :

- the name of the interviewer (an Interviewer's Identity Card must be shown if face to face);
- an assurance that the interview will be carried out according to the MRS Code of Conduct;
- the general subject of the interview;
- the purpose of the interview;
- if asked, the likely length of the interview;
- any costs likely to be incurred by the Respondent.

B22 Respondents (including employees in employee research) must not be unduly pressurised to participate.

B23 Members must delete any responses given by the Respondent, if requested, and if this is reasonable and practicable.

B24 Recruiters/interviewers must not reveal to any other Respondents the detailed answers provided by any Respondent or the identity of any other Respondent interviewed.

Incentives

B25 Where incentives are offered, Members must clearly inform the Respondent who will administer the incentive.
Comment: Incentives need not be of a monetary nature to be acceptable to a Respondent as a token of appreciation.
With the Client's permission, an offer to supply the Respondent with a brief summary report of the project's findings can sometimes prove a better alternative encouragement to participate in a research project. Other alternatives are for example:

- *charity donations;*
- *non-monetary gifts;*
- *prize draws (for prize draws the rules, as detailed in the MRS Prize Draws Guidance Note, must be adhered to).*

Children

Comment: The intention of the following provisions regarding the age of Respondents is to protect children who are potentially vulnerable members of society and to strengthen the principle of public trust.

B26 Consent of a parent or responsible adult (acting in loco parentis) must be obtained before interviewing a child under 16 in the following circumstances:

- in home/at home (face-to-face and telephone interviewing);
- group discussions/depth interviews;
- postal questionnaires;

- internet questionnaires;
- e-mail;
- where interviewer and child are alone together;
- in public places such as in-street/in-store/central locations (see exception under B27).

B27 Interviews being conducted in public places, such as in-street/in-store/central locations, with 14 year olds or over, may take place without consent of a parent or responsible adult. In these situations Members must give an explanatory thank you note to the child.
Comment: Under special circumstances, permission to waive parental consent may be obtained, but only with the prior approval of the MRS Market Research Standards Board.

B28 Where the consent of a parent or responsible adult is required Members must ensure that the adult is given sufficient information about the nature of the research to enable them to provide informed consent.

B29 Members must ensure that the parent or responsible adult giving consent is recorded (by name, relationship or role).

B30 For self-completion postal questionnaires, Members must ensure that:

- when it is known (or ought reasonably to be known) that all or a majority of Respondents are likely to be under 16, these are addressed to the parent or responsible adult; and
- when it is known (or ought reasonably to be known) that all or a majority of Respondents are likely to be under 16, all questionnaires carry a note or notice explaining that consent is required for all children to participate.

B31 For research administered electronically over the internet, when it is known (or ought reasonably to be known) that all or a majority of Respondents are likely to be under 16, Members must ensure that Respondents are asked to give their age before any other personal information is requested. Further, if the age given is under 16, the child must be excluded from giving further personal information until the appropriate consent from a parent or responsible adult has been obtained.

B32 In all cases, Members must ensure that a child has an opportunity to decline to take part, even though a parent or a responsible adult has given consent on their behalf. This remains the case if the research takes place in school.

B33 Personal information relating to other people must not be collected from children unless for the purposes of gaining consent from a parent or a responsible adult.

Qualitative Research

B34 At the time of recruitment (or before the research takes place if details change after recruitment), Members must ensure that Respondents are told all relevant information as per rule B21 and:

- the location of the discussion and if it is to take place in a viewing facility;
- whether observers are likely to be present;
- when and how the discussion is to be recorded;
- the likely length of the discussion including the start and finish time; and
- the Member, moderator and/or research agency that will be conducting the research.

B35 Members must ensure that completed recruitment questionnaires, incentive and attendance lists, or any other research information which identifies Respondents, are not passed to Clients without the explicit permission of the Respondents; and Members must take reasonable steps to ensure that the documents are used only for the purpose agreed at the time of data collection.

B36 If Members have agreed with Clients that observers are to be present, Members must inform all observers fully about their legal and ethical responsibilities.

B37 Members must make clear to Respondents the capacity in which observers are present; Clients must be presented as such, even if they are also Researchers and/or Members of MRS.
Comment: This also applies to Members themselves when an employee of a Client organisation, advertising/design/PR agency etc.

B38 There are some situations where observers could adversely affect Respondents' interests and/or wellbeing, and in such instances, Members must ensure that Respondents are told at an appropriate stage the identity of any observer who might be present at the discussion or interview.

B39 Members must ensure that, in instances where observers may know Respondents (as may occur in business-to-business research), Respondents are informed before the start that their interviews are to be observed, with a warning that the observers may include Clients who already know them.

B40 The issue of anonymity and recognition is a particular problem in business and employee research. If guarantees cannot be given then Members must ensure that observers are fully introduced before the group/interview begins and Respondents given a chance to withdraw.

B41 Members must ensure that Respondents on attendance at a venue are informed about the nature of any observation, monitoring or recording and Respondents are given the option of withdrawing from the group/interview.

B42 Members must ensure that any material handed to Clients or included in reports, without consent from Respondents, is anonymised eg transcripts containing verbatim comments and projective material.
Comment: Special care must be taken when the universe is small, as in the case of some business-to-business research studies.

Mystery Shopping

Comment: The objective of a mystery customer research project is to provide management information on processes and/or quality of service, in order to aid training and retraining plans, improvements in service and hence increase customer satisfaction etc.

For mystery shopping exercises the 'Respondent' will be a staff member who is subject to the mystery shop and as such there are different levels of allowable disclosure and data usage.

B43 For mystery shopping of a Client's own organisation, Members must take reasonable steps to ensure that:

- the Client's employees have been advised by their employer that their service delivery may be checked through mystery shopping;
- the objectives and intended uses of the results have been made clear by the employer to staff (including the level of reporting if at branch/store or individual level); and
- if mystery shopping is to be used in relation to any employment terms and conditions, this has been made clear by the employer.

B44 Since competitors' employees cannot be advised that they may be mystery shopped, Members must ensure that their identities are not revealed. Members must ensure that employees are not recorded (eg by using audio, photographic or video equipment). This applies in all instances where employees cannot be or have not been advised that they could be mystery shopped.

B45 Where there is mystery shopping of a Client's agents or authorised distributors (as well as any organisations which are responsible to a compliance authority), Members must ensure that:

- the employees to be mystery shopped have been advised by their employer and/or regulator that their service delivery and/or regulatory compliance may be checked by mystery shopping;
- the objectives and intended uses of the results have been made clear by the employer and/or regulator (including the level of reporting if at branch/store or individual level); and
- if mystery shopping is to be used in relation to any employment/contractual/regulatory terms and conditions this has been made clear by the employer and/or regulator.

B46 Members must take reasonable steps to ensure that mystery shoppers are fully informed of the implications and protected from any adverse implications of conducting a mystery shopping exercise.

Comment: For example, they must be made aware by the Member that their identity may be revealed to the organisation/individual being mystery shopped if they use personal cards to make purchases, loan arrangements etc and credit ratings may be affected.

Observation

B47 Members must ensure that all of the following are undertaken when observation equipment is being used:

- clear and legible signs must be placed in areas where surveillance is taking place;
- cameras must be sited so that they monitor only the areas intended for surveillance.
- signs must state the individual/organisation responsible for the surveillance, including contact information and the purpose of the observation.

Comment: Rule A10 of the Code requires Members to take all reasonable precautions to ensure that Respondents are not harmed or adversely affected as a result of participating in a research project. This may have particular pertinence in an ethnographic and observational setting. Issues to be considered are:

- *the need to be sensitive to the possibility that their presence may, at times, be seen as an unwarranted intrusion; here safeguards, and the ability to end the observation quickly, must be built into any ethnographic situation;*
- *the need to be sensitive to the possibility that Respondents may become over involved with them at a personal level; and*
- *the need to be sensitive to the possibility of 'observation fatigue'; again there is value in having the ability to end the observation quickly within any ethnographic situation.*

Using Research Techniques for Non-Research Purposes

B48 Members must adhere to the rules in the separate regulations, *Using Research Techniques for Non-Research Purposes,* when conducting exercises which are for purposes in addition to, or other than, research.

Analysis and Reporting of Research Findings

B49 Members must ensure that research conclusions disseminated by them are clearly and adequately supported by the data.

B50 Members must comply with reasonable requests to make available to anyone the technical information necessary to assess the validity of any published findings from a research project.

B51 Members must ensure that their names, or those of their employer, are only used in connection with any research project as an assurance that the latter has been carried out in conformity with the Code if they are satisfied on reasonable grounds that the project has in all respects met the Code's requirements.

B52 Members must allow Clients to arrange checks on the quality of fieldwork and data preparation provided that the Client pays any additional costs involved in this.

B53 Members must provide Clients with sufficient technical details to enable Clients to assess the validity of results of research projects carried out on their behalf.

B54 Members must ensure that data tables include sufficient technical information to enable reasonable interpretation of the validity of the results.

B55 Members must ensure that reports include sufficient information to enable reasonable interpretation of the validity of the results.

B56 Members must ensure that reports and presentations clearly distinguish between facts and interpretation.

B57 Members must ensure that when interpreting data they make clear which data they are using to support their interpretation.

B58 Members must ensure that qualitative reports and presentations accurately reflect the findings of the research in addition to the research practitioner's interpretations and conclusions.

B59 Members must take reasonable steps to check and where necessary amend any Client-prepared materials prior to publication to ensure that the published research results will not be incorrectly or misleadingly reported.
Comment: This means that Members are expected to take reasonable steps to ensure that any press releases include either final report details (including question wording for any questions quoted) or details of where the information can be obtained (eg via a website link).

B60 Members must take reasonable steps to ensure that findings from a research project, published by themselves or in their employer's name, are not incorrectly or misleadingly presented.

B61 If Members are aware, or ought reasonably to be aware, that findings from a research project have been incorrectly or misleadingly reported by a Client he/she must at the earliest opportunity:

■ refuse permission for the Client to use their name further in connection with the incorrect or misleading published findings; and

■ publish in an appropriate forum the relevant technical details of the project to correct any incorrect or misleading reporting.

Data Storage

B62 Members must take reasonable steps to ensure that all hard copy and electronic lists containing personal data are held securely in accordance with the relevant data retention policies and/or contractual obligations.

B63 Members must take reasonable steps to ensure that all parties involved in the research are aware of their obligations regarding security of data.

B64 Members must take reasonable steps to ensure that the destruction of data is adequate for the confidentiality of the data being destroyed. For example, any personal data must be destroyed in a manner which safeguards confidentiality.

APPENDIX: ICC/ESOMAR CODE OF MARKETING AND SOCIAL RESEARCH PRACTICE

The MRS Code of Conduct is based upon the principles of the ICC/ES-OMAR Code whilst taking account of UK legislation and practice. The ICC/ESOMAR Code is included for reference only. All disciplinary and compliance enforcement will be in relation to the MRS Code of Conduct.

A. General

1. Marketing research must always be carried out objectively and in accordance with established scientific principles.
2. Marketing research must always conform to the national and international legislation which applies in those countries involved in a given research project.

B. The Rights of Respondents

3. Respondents' cooperation in a marketing research project is entirely voluntary at all stages. They must not be misled when being asked for their cooperation.
4. Respondents' anonymity must be strictly preserved. If the Respondent on request from the Researcher has given permission for data to be passed on in a form which allows that Respondent to be personally identified:

(a) the Respondent must first have been told to whom the information would be supplied and the purposes for which it will be used, and also
(b) the Researcher must ensure that the information will not be used for any non-research purpose and that the recipient of the information has agreed to conform to the requirements of this Code.

5. The Researcher must take all reasonable precautions to ensure that Respondents are in no way directly harmed or adversely affected as a result of their participation in a marketing research project.
6. The Researcher must take special care when interviewing children and young people. The informed consent of the parent or responsible adult must first be obtained for interviews with children.
7. Respondents must be told (normally at the beginning of the interview) if observation techniques or recording equipment are being used,

except where these are used in a public place. If a Respondent so wishes, the record or relevant section of it must be destroyed or deleted. Respondents' anonymity must not be infringed by the use of such methods.

8. Respondents must be enabled to check without difficulty the identity and bona fides of the Researcher.

C. The Professional Responsibilities of Researchers

9. Researchers must not, whether knowingly or negligently, act in any way which could bring discredit on the marketing research profession or lead to a loss of public confidence in it.

10. Researchers must not make false claims about their skills and experience or about those of their organisation.

11. Researchers must not unjustifiably criticise or disparage other Researchers.

12. Researchers must always strive to design research which is cost-efficient and of adequate quality, and then to carry this out to the specifications agreed with the Client.

13. Researchers must ensure the security of all research records in their possession.

14. Researchers must not knowingly allow the dissemination of conclusions from a marketing research project which are not adequately supported by the data. They must always be prepared to make available the technical information necessary to assess the validity of any published findings.

15. When acting in their capacity as Researchers the latter must not undertake any non-research activities, for example database marketing, involving data about individuals which will be used for direct marketing and promotional activities. Any such non-research activities must always, in the way they are organised and carried out, be clearly differentiated from marketing research activities.

D. The Mutual Rights and Responsibilities of Researchers and Clients

16. These rights and responsibilities will normally be governed by a written Contract between the Researcher and the Client. The parties may amend the provisions of Rules 19–23 below if they have agreed to this in writing beforehand; but the other requirements of this Code may not be altered in this way. Marketing research must also always be

conducted according to the principles of fair competition, as generally understood and accepted.

17. The Researcher must inform the Client if the work to be carried out for that Client is to be combined or syndicated in the same project with work for other Clients but must not disclose the identity of such Clients.

18. The Researcher must inform the Client as soon as possible in advance when any part of the work for that Client is to be subcontracted outside the Researcher's own organisation (including the use of any outside consultants). On request the Client must be told the identity of any such subcontractor.

19. The Client does not have the right, without prior agreement between the parties involved, to exclusive use of the Researcher's services or those of his organisation, whether in whole or in part. In carrying out work for different Clients, however, the Researcher must endeavour to avoid possible clashes of interest between the services provided to those Clients.

20. The following Records remain the property of the Client and must not be disclosed by the Researcher to any third party without the Client's permission:

(a) Marketing research briefs, specifications and other information provided by the Client.

(b) The research data and findings from a marketing research project (except in the case of syndicated or multi-client projects or services where the same data are available to more than one Client).

The Client has however no right to know the names or addresses of Respondents unless the latter's explicit permission for this has first been obtained by the Researcher (this particular requirement cannot be altered under Rule 16).

21. Unless it is specifically agreed to the contrary, the following Records remain the property of the Researcher:

(a) Marketing research proposals and cost quotations (unless these have been paid for by the Client). They must not be disclosed by the Client to any third party, other than to a consultant working for the Client on that project (with the exception of any consultant working also for a competitor of the Researcher). In particular, they must not be used by the Client to influence research proposals or cost quotations from other Researchers.

(b) The contents of a report in the case of syndicated and/or multi-client projects or services where the same data are available to more than one Client and where it is clearly understood that the resulting reports are available for general purchase or subscription. The Client may not disclose the findings of such research to any third party (other than to his own consultants and advisors for use in connection with his business) without the permission of the Researcher.

(c) All other research Records prepared by the Researcher (with the exception in the case of non-syndicated projects of the report to the Client, and also the research design and questionnaire where the costs of developing these are covered by the charges paid by the Client).

22. The Researcher must conform to currently agreed professional practice relating to the keeping of such Records for an appropriate period of time after the end of the project. On request the Researcher must supply the Client with duplicate copies of such Records provided that such duplicates do not breach anonymity and confidentiality requirements (Rule 4); that the request is made within the agreed time limit for keeping the Records; and that the Client pays the reasonable costs of providing the duplicates.

23. The Researcher must not disclose the identity of the Client (provided there is no legal obligation to do so), or any confidential information about the latter's business, to any third party without the Client's permission.

24. The Researcher must on request allow the Client to arrange for checks on the quality of fieldwork and data preparation provided that the Client pays any additional costs involved in this. Any such checks must conform to the requirements of Rule 4.

25. The Researcher must provide the Client with all appropriate technical details of any research project carried out for that Client.

26. When reporting on the results of a marketing research project the Researcher must make a clear distinction between the findings as such, the Researcher's interpretation of these and any recommendations based on them.

27. Where any of the findings of a research project are published by the Client the latter has a responsibility to ensure that these are not misleading. The Researcher must be consulted and agree in advance the form and content of publication, and must take action to correct any misleading statements about the research and its findings.

28. Researchers must not allow their names to be used in connection with any research project as an assurance that the latter has been carried out in conformity with this Code unless they are confident that the project has in all respects met the Code's requirements.

29. Researchers must ensure that Clients are aware of the existence of this Code and of the need to comply with its requirements.

Appendix 3: Conducting research with employees

INTRODUCTION

These Guidelines interpret the MRS Code of Conduct (revised 2005) and provide additional best practice guidance. Unless otherwise stated, Guidelines are not binding.

They should be read in conjunction with other MRS guidelines, particularly the Mystery Customer Research Guidelines, since this type of research covers another aspect of monitoring of employees. The main aim of these guidelines is to ensure that research is transparent to employees in order to promote public support for market research. More generally, they seek to promote professionalism in the conduct of employee research.

The general public and other interested parties are entitled to complete assurance that every research project is carried out in accordance with the Code of Conduct and that their rights and privacy are respected.

Rules from the Code of Conduct applicable in each section of this document are headed 'The Rules'. These rules are binding on MRS members and breaches may result in disciplinary action. The guidance that follows the rules provides interpretation and additional best practice. Members are reminded that this document is designed to complement the MRS Code of Conduct and should not be consulted in isolation.

As specified in the Code, it is the responsibility of the researcher to keep abreast of any legislation which could affect research with employees and to ensure that all those involved in a project are aware of and agree to abide by the MRS Code of Conduct.

This material is provided for information only. It is not legal advice and should not be relied upon as such. Specific legal advice should be taken in relation to specific issues.

MRS would like to thank Peter Goudge for his co-authorship of this guidance, and also for the help and advice of the many members of the MRS Employee Research Group (ERG) who have contributed to the various editions of this guideline over the years.

DEFINITION OF EMPLOYEE RESEARCH

The 'discipline' of employee research is any formalised activity developed to gather information about the opinions and behaviours of employees. It is the exploration of aspects of an individual's working life with an employer – what they do as well as what they think. Rather than seeing it as an isolated practice, this broad definition seeks to place employee research within the wider framework of two-way internal communications and effective Human Resource Management, in which we see it as playing an integral part.

Please note that the word 'interview' is used generically in this document to cover the process whereby information is gathered from respondents, even though a considerable amount of this type of research is conducted on a self-completion basis whether on paper or electronically via e-mail, intranets and the internet.

RELATIONSHIP WITH DATA PROTECTION

All personal employee data is covered by the Data Protection Act 1998. For full details of the implications of the Act on employer/employee relationships see the Information Commissioner's publications on employment. Details are available via www.ico.gov.uk in the Codes of Practice section of the website.

GUIDELINES

1. Planning a Quantitative Study
A. Communication with Employees
The Rules

A3   Members must act honestly in dealings with Respondents, Clients (actual or potential), employers, employees, sub-contractors and the general public.

B2   All written or oral assurances made by any Member involved in commissioning or conducting projects must be factually correct and honoured by the Member.

B21   Members must ensure that all of the following are clearly communicated to the Respondent:

- the name of the interviewer (an Interviewer's Identity Card must be shown if face to face);
- an assurance that the interview will be carried out according to the MRS Code of Conduct;
- the general subject of the interview;
- the purpose of the interview;
- if asked, the likely length of the interview;
- any costs likely to be incurred by the Respondent.

B22   Respondents (including employees in employee research) must not be unduly pressurised to participate.

Guidance

1. Prior publicity is important to help boost rates of response. Any number of media can be deployed to advise employees of the research and its purpose – ranging from in-house magazines and personal briefings to videos and posters as well as e-mail and the intranet.
2. A letter from a relevant person with authority should be sent prior to the research, or at the time the research is conducted.
3. In accordance with rule B2, any assurances made in communications with staff regarding the research (such as anonymity) must be honoured.
4. Employees should be informed as to how it is intended that the results from the research will be used; and, where relevant, examples of how results from previous studies have been acted upon. Such information will help to encourage participation.

B. Sample Selection
The Rules

B8 The anonymity of Respondents must be preserved unless they have given their informed consent for their details to be revealed or for attributable comments to be passed on.
Comment: Members must be particularly careful if sample sizes are very small (such as in business and employee research) that they do not inadvertently identify organisations or departments and therefore individuals.

B9 If Respondents have given consent for data to be passed on in a form which allows them to be personally identified, Members must:

- demonstrate that they have taken all reasonable steps to ensure that it will only be used for the purpose for which it was collected; and
- fully inform Respondents as to what will be revealed, to whom and for what purpose.

B10 If Respondents request individual complaints or unresolved issues to be passed back to a Client (for example in customer satisfaction research), Members must comply with that request. The comments/issues to be passed back to a Client must be agreed with the Respondent and must not be linked back to any other data or used for any other purpose without the explicit consent of the Respondent.

B18 A Respondent's right to withdraw from a research project at any stage must be respected.

B23 Members must delete any responses given by the Respondent, if requested, and if this is reasonable and practicable.

Guidance

1. To avoid skewed or unrepresentative data in quantitative studies, selection should be arranged to ensure that each sample represents a balanced cross-section of the whole. This can be achieved either by drawing a random sample (eg selecting every nth name from an alphabetical list of employees), or by setting quotas (eg a representative proportion of the whole according to sub-groups such as department, job grade, age, working locations etc).

2. Sample sizes in specialised areas may be very small to the point where employees themselves could be identified. If there is a reasonable risk of an employee being identified, due to the sample size of the population or sub-population being covered, the employee should be informed of this risk at the beginning of the interview and given the opportunity to withdraw.

3. On some occasions employees may want requests or additional comments passed back to an employer. In these circumstances, in

accordance with rule B10, the relevant comments must not be linked back to any other data unless agreed. The researcher must honour any promises made eg to pass the information to the employer for resolution.

4. Where the universe of respondents is small, and the respondents may be well known to the client, special precautions should be taken to comply with B8. All information provided to the client should be checked to ensure that respondents cannot be identified – this includes the selection of any verbatim comments from depths or groups that they may wish to use in a presentation or report.

2. The Research

A: Qualitative Research

The Rules

B15 If there is to be any recording, monitoring or observation during an interview, Respondents must be informed about this both at recruitment and at the beginning of the interview.

B17 Respondents must not be misled when being asked for cooperation to participate in a research project.

B18 A Respondent's right to withdraw from a research project at any stage must be respected.

B34 At the time of recruitment (or before the research takes place if details change after recruitment), Members must ensure that Respondents are told all relevant information as per rule B21 and:

- the location of the discussion and if it is to take place in a viewing facility;
- whether observers are likely to be present;
- when and how the discussion is to be recorded;
- the likely length of the discussion including the start and finish time;
- the Member, moderator and/or research agency that will be conducting the research.

B37 Members must make clear to Respondents the capacity in which observers are present; Clients must be presented as such, even if they are also Researchers and/or Members of MRS.

Guidance

1. Researchers should reassure employees of the confidentiality of anything they may say in a group or depth interview.

2. In accordance with rule B15, the researcher must inform employees about any recording or monitoring methods (eg tape recording, video recording, and presence of a mirror or a camera) both at recruitment

and at the beginning of an interview, giving the employee the option not to proceed. This also applies to instances where remote monitoring is used. Employees may prefer groups to be recorded and transcribed and researchers should give employees this option.

3. Where permission is to be obtained to release digital, audio or video recordings, the researcher should ensure that employees are given as much relevant information as possible about the future use of the data, in particular:

- to whom they are to be given;
- to whom they are likely to be shown;
- for what purposes they are likely to be used.

4. In the same way that employees are given the opportunity to withdraw at the recruitment stage or at the start of a group or depth interview if it is going to be recorded, they should similarly be given the opportunity to withdraw should other people from the company (eg senior managers, HR personnel) who are not selected respondents intend to be present.

5. Given the sensitivities of conducting research amongst employees, only in exceptional circumstances should groups or depth interviews be observed or video recorded.

B: Online (E-mail and Web-based) Research
The Rules

B8   The anonymity of Respondents must be preserved unless they have given their informed consent for their details to be revealed or for attributable comments to be passed on.
Comment: Members must be particularly careful if sample sizes are very small (such as in business and employee research) that they do not inadvertently identify organisations or departments and therefore individuals.

Guidance

1. When research documentation is distributed electronically and employees are required to complete it onscreen, researchers should take into account any limits on the employee's privacy when answering, and how this might impact on the validity of the research results.
2. Research documentation sent out as attachments should be piloted on the employer's network. This will ensure that they can get through security barriers or firewall and identify any problems with either the layout or appearance of the documentation by virtue of the equipment (eg PC) and software available to the employee.

3. If some form of tracking is used (to ensure that employees do not submit more than one response) it should be undertaken by the researcher and not the employer.

4. Researchers should take the following issues into account when deciding on whether an online approach is the best methodology to use. These include:

- access: How many people use e-mail/the intranet/internet? How many have individual access? Do they have internet access?
- user confidence: How new is e-mail/the intranet/internet? Are they used daily? Are all employees equally confident using these channels?
- confidentiality: How much concern is there? How much reassurance is needed? Would a password ease (or exacerbate) these concerns?

5. Although online research affords the possibility of requiring respondents to answer a question before moving on, this capability should not be deployed in areas such as profiling or demographic questions which could raise concerns about the identification of individuals.

3: Reporting the Results

The Rules

B8 The anonymity of Respondents must be preserved unless they have given their informed consent for their details to be revealed or for attributable comments to be passed on.
Comment: Members must be particularly careful if sample sizes are very small (such as in business and employee research) that they do not inadvertently identify organisations or departments and therefore individuals.

B42 Members must ensure that any material handed to Clients or included in reports, without consent from Respondents, is anonymised eg transcripts containing verbatim comments and projective material.
Comment: Special care must be taken when the universe is small, as in the case of some business to business research studies.

Guidance

1. The employer should be made aware before a project has started what employee information can be detailed in the report. Only in instances where an employee has given permission can their name be revealed.

2. In accordance with rule B8, care must be taken when the range of employees to be interviewed is limited by job title such that by identifying the department or the local region, the identity of the employee is

disclosed or potentially disclosed. Wherever there is a conflict of interest between a researcher's duty and obligation to employees and/or to employers, the duty and obligation to employees is paramount.

3. It is recommended that reports should only examine the results of sub-groups where 10 or more have responded to the research.

4. Due to the nature of employee research there is a higher possibility that employees will be contacted on a regular basis. Therefore, research documentation should be clear, relevant and logical to avoid employee fatigue. (See the MRS Questionnaire Design Guidelines for guidance in this area.)

5. Researchers should agree in advance with the client as to how employee complaints about internal company matters are to be handled. As a general rule, researchers should only pass back complaints at a very general level of detail, given that the complaints will have been made anonymously. Anonymous allegations made in the course of a research project should not be the sole grounds for disciplinary action against a named employee. Rather, they should be a starting point for an investigation by the employer, if it is warranted.

References

Argyris, C (1960) *Understanding Organizational Behaviour*, Dorsey Press, Homewood, Ill

Australian Workplace [accessed January 2005] CEA and Compass case studies [Online] http://www.workplace.gov.au/WP/Content/Files/WP/WR/General/CEA_case_study.pdf

Baker Tilly [accessed May 2005] AIM High [Online] http://www.growingbusiness.co.uk/YfnFQ0toW_iRGA.html

Barrow, S (1996) Understanding people at work – a new priority for researchers? paper presented to the Market Research Society Conference

Bitner, M J, Booms, B H and Mohr, L A (1994) Critical service encounters: the employees viewpoint, *Journal of Marketing*, **58** (October), pp 95–106

Brace, I (2004) *Questionnaire Design*, Kogan Page, London

Burke, W and Litwin, G (1992) A causal model of organizational performance and change, *Journal of Management*, **18** (3), pp 523–45

Business in the Community [accessed February 2005] *Corporate Responsibility Index* [Online] http://www.bitc.org.uk/programmes/key_initiatives/corporate_responsibility_index/

Chartered Institute of Personnel and Development (CIPD) [accessed May 2005] *Human Capital* [Online] http://www.cipd.co.uk/research/_humcap.htm?IsSrchRes=1

CIPD (2004) [accessed April 2005] *People and Technology: Is HR getting the best out of IT?* [Online] http://www.cipd.co.uk/NR/rdonlyres/328BDDEC-2C70-4120-92E9- A4EE6E86090D/0/3081peopletechsurv04.pdf

Cranfield School of Management [accessed March 2005] *Managing and Measuring for Value: The case of call centre performance* [Online] http://www.som.cranfield.ac.uk/som/news/resources/callcentreperformance.pdf

Czepiel, J A (1990) Service encounters and service relationships: implications for research, *Journal of Business Research*, **20**, pp 13–21

Deming, W E (1986) Out of the Crisis, MIT Press, Cambridge, Mass

References

Department for Trade and Industry (2003) [accessed April 2005] European Works Councils [Online] http://www.dti.gov.uk/er/europe/ewcdoc.pdf

Dorgan, M (2003) [accessed April 2005] Employee as customer: lessons from marketing and IT, *PA Consulting* [Online] http://www.paconsulting.com/news/by_pa/2003/by_pa_20030101.htm

Drucker, P (2001) *The Essential Drucker*, Harper Collins, New York

European Foundation for Quality Management [accessed January 2005] *Excellence Model* [Online] http://www.efqm.org/Default.aspx?tabid=35

Fairhurst, D [accessed April 2005] *Evolving a Successful Recruitment Policy: Lessons for the recruitment industry* [Online] http://www.recruitmentsociety.org.uk/display_article.asp?id=32

Farner, S, Luthans, F and Sommer, S M (2001) An empirical assessment of internal customer service, *Managing Service Quality*, **11** (5), pp 350–58

Gattorna, J L [accessed May 2005] Keynote address to Logistics Ireland 2003 Supply Chain Management Forum [Online] http://www.nitl.ie/hdocs/chainmgt/present_2003.cfm

Gittell, J H (2003) *The Southwest Airlines Way: Using the power of relationships to achieve high performance*, McGraw-Hill, New York

Greenway, G and Southgate, P (1985) Quality of research in the customer-banker relationship: match or mis- match, paper presented to the Market Research Society Conference

Guest, D E and Conway, N (2002) *Pressure at Work and the Psychological Contract*, CIPD, London

Harrington, H James (1998) [accessed January 2005] Happy employees don't equal happy customers, *Quality Digest* [Online] http://www.qualitydigest.com/june98/html/perfimp.html

Harrington, H J (1999) [accessed January 2005] Happy employees don't equal happy customers part II, *Quality Digest* [Online] http://www.qualitydigest.com/jan99/html/body_perfrmnce.html

Hay Group (2001) [accessed February 2005] *The Retention Dilemma* [Online] http://www.haygroup.co.uk/Expertise/downloads/Retention_Dilemma.pdf

Health and Safety Executive [accessed April 2005] *Work-Related Stress* [Online] http://www.hse.gov.uk/stress/index.htm

Heskett, J L, Sasser, W E and Schlesinger L A (1997) *The Value Profit Chain*, Free Press, New York

Hill, N [accessed March 2005] *Does Customer Satisfaction Pay?* [Online] http://www.saferpak.com/csm_articles/Loyalty%204%20Does%20customer%20satisfaction%20pay.pdf

Infoquest [accessed February 2005] *Employee Satisfaction and Opinion Surveys* [Online] http://www.infoquestcrm.co.uk/employee_surveys.html

Jamieson, D and Richards, T (1996) Committed employees – the key focus in strategic development, paper presented to the Market Research Society Conference

John Lewis Partnership [accessed March 2005] About Us [Online] http://www.johnlewispartnership.co.uk/TemplatePage.aspx?PageType=ARA&PageID=1

Johnson, J (2000) Differences in supervisor and non-supervisor perceptions of quality culture and organizational climate, *Public Personnel Management*, **29** (1), pp 119–28

Judge, T A, Bono, J E and Locke, E A (2000) Personality and job satisfaction: the mediating role of job characteristics, *Journal of Applied Psychology*, **85**, pp 237–49

Kaplan, R and Norton, D (1992) The balanced scorecard: measures that drive performance, *Harvard Business Review*, **70** (1), pp 71–79

Koys, D J (2001) The effects of employee satisfaction, organisational citizenship behaviour, and turnover on organisational effectiveness: a unit-level, longitudinal study, *Personnel Psychology*, **54**, pp 101–14

Kruse, D and Blasi, J (2000) [accessed March 2005] *Employee Ownership and Corporate Performance* [Online] http://www.nceo.org/library/corpperf.html

LePree, J (2003) [accessed January 2005] Staying ahead of the curve, *MSI NewsLine Weekly*, 21 April [Online] http://www.manufacturingsystems.com/newsletter/042103/sb0421.asp

Levering, R (2004) [accessed January 2005] Transforming your organization: creating a great place to work, Building Trust Conference, Washington, DC, 14 April [Online] http://www.winningworkplaces.org/library/research/advantages.php#100best

Likert, R (1932) A technique for the measurement of attitudes, *Archives of Psychology*, **140**, pp 5–55

Madigan, C O [accessed April 2005] How three companies are leveraging intellectual capital to achieve strategic goals, with quotes from G Petrash and S Wallman, *Business Finance* [Online] http://www.bfmag.com/channels/businessStrategy/article.html?articleID=5356

Market Research Society (MRS) [accessed 11 November 2005] *Code of Conduct* [Online] http://www.mrs.org.uk/code.htm

MRS [accessed 11 November 2005] *Internet Research Guidelines* [Online] http://www.mrs.org.uk/standards/internet.htm

Mayo, A (2001) *The Human Value of the Enterprise: Valuing people as assets – monitoring, measuring, managing*, Nicholas Brealey, London

McClymont, L and Briggs, T (1999) Getting employees on our side, paper presented to the Market Research Society Conference

McNeil, R (1993) Staff research and Total Quality Management – looking in the mirror, paper presented to the ESOMAR Congress

Mondragon Corporacion Cooperativa [accessed March 2005] *The History of an Experience* [Online] http://www.mondragon.mcc.es/ing/quienessomos/historia.html

National Whistleblower Center [accessed April 2005] *Labor Day Report* [Online] http://www.whistleblowers.org/labordayreport.htm

Neely, A, Gray, D, Kennerley, M and Marr, B (2002) [accessed April 2005] Measuring corporate management and leadership *capability, Council for Excellence in Management and Leadership (CEML)* [Online] http://www.som.cranfield.ac.uk/som/research/centres/cbp/downloads/CEML%20Report.pdf

References

Organ, D W (1988) *Organizational Citizenship Behavior: The good soldier syndrome*, Lexington Books, Lexington, Mass

Orwell, G (1949) 1984, Secker and Warburg, London

Paton, S (1999) [accessed January 2005] Unhappy employees and unhappy customers, *Quality Digest* [Online] http://www.qualitydigest.com/jan99/html/body_frstwrd.html

Patterson, M, West, M, Lawthom, R and Nickell, S (1997) [accessed March 2005] Do employee attitudes predict company performance? *FMI Brief*, November [Online] http://www.som.cranfield.ac.uk/som/research/centres/cbp/whatsnew/KNOWLED2.HTM

Reichheld, F (1996) The Loyalty Effect: *The hidden force behind growth, profits, and lasting value*, Harvard Business School Press, Boston, Mass

Reynolds, K E and Beatty, S E (1999) Customer benefits and company consequences of customer- salesperson relationships in retailing, *Journal of Retailing*, **75** (1), pp 11–32

Robinson, D, Perryman, S and Hayday, S (2004) *The Drivers of Employee Engagement*, IES Report 408, Institute for Employment Studies, Brighton

Robinson, S L (1996) Trust and breach of the psychological contract, *Administrative Science Quarterly*, **41**, pp 575–99

Rogelberg, S, Luong, A, Sederburg, M and Cristol, D (2000) Employee attitude surveys: examining the attitudes of noncompliant employees, *Journal of Applied Psychology*, **85** (2), pp 284–93

Rucci, A J, Kirn, S P and Quinn, R T (1998) The employee–customer profit chain at Sears, *Harvard Business Review*, **76** (1), pp 83–97

Ryan, A M, Schmidt, M J and Johnson, R H (1996) Attitudes and effectiveness: examining relations at an organizational level, *Personnel Psychology*, **49** (4), pp 853–82

Schlackman, W, Thornley, R and Vuillamy, J (1970) The Hartcliffe Project – a progress report of a sociological study in environmental planning, paper presented to the Market Research Society Conference

Sheldon, R, Heywood, C, Turner, J and Gutmann, J (1996) The assessment of London Transport staff preferences for investment, paper presented to the Market Research Society Conference

Sinclair, R and Lavis, C (2001) [accessed January 2005] Miserable staff are more productive, *Personnel Today* [Online] http://www.personneltoday.com/Articles/2001/06/13/6741/Miserable+staff+are+more+productive.htm

Stewart, T A (1997) *Intellectual Capital: The new wealth of organizations*, Doubleday, New York

Stone, M, Bond, A and Foss, B (2004) *Consumer Insight*, Kogan Page, London

Sveiby, K E [accessed March 2005] *The Invisible Balance Sheet* [Online] http://www.sveiby.com/articles/InvisibleBalance.html

Teer, F (1979) Information for management, paper presented to the ESOMAR Congress

Towers Perrin (2004) [accessed February 2005] Profitability is linked to employee engagement, *Personnel Today* [Online] http://www.personneltoday.co.uk/Articles/2004/12/17/27188/Profitability+is+linked+to+employee+engagement.htm

Tuckman, B W (1965) Developmental sequence in small groups, *Psychological Bulletin*, **63**, pp 384–99

Watson Wyatt [accessed January 2005] *Employee-Friendly Workplaces Get Dramatically Greater Returns for Shareholders* [Online] http://www.winningworkplaces.org/library/research/advantages.php#friendly

Watson Wyatt [accessed March 2005] *WorkUSA(r) 2004/2005: Effective employees drive financial results* [Online] http://www.watsonwyatt.com/research/resrender.asp?id=w-788&page=1

White, M (2001) [accessed April 2005] *Women with Children Working Longer Hours* [Online] http://www.esrc.ac.uk/esrccontent/news/sep8.asp

Wills, S and Williams, P (2004) Insight as a strategic asset – the opportunity and the stark reality, paper presented to the Market Research Society Conference

Worcester, R M (1973) A new look at research among employees, paper presented to the Market Research Society Conference

Index

ALSO AVAILABLE FROM KOGAN PAGE IN THE MARKET RESEARCH IN PRACTICE SERIES: